The Indian
Independence
Act of 1947

MILESTONES

IN MODERN
WORLD HISTORY

The Boer War

The Bolshevik
Revolution

The British
Industrial Revolution

The Chinese
Cultural Revolution

The Collapse of
the Soviet Union

The Congress of Vienna

The Cuban Revolution

D-Day and the
Liberation of France

The End of Apartheid
in South Africa

The Establishment
of the State of Israel

The French Revolution
and the Rise
of Napoleon

The Great Irish Famine

The Indian
Independence
Act of 1947

The Iranian Revolution

The Manhattan Project

The Marshall Plan

The Mexican
Revolution

The Treaty of Nanking

The Treaty of Versailles

The Universal
Declaration of
Human Rights

The Indian Independence Act of 1947

SUSAN MUADDI DARRAJ

CHELSEA HOUSE
An Infobase Learning Company

The Indian Independence Act of 1947

Copyright © 2011 by Infobase Learning

Chelsea House
An imprint of Infobase Learning
132 West 31st Street
New York, NY 10001

Library of Congress Cataloging-in-Publication Data

Darraj, Susan Muaddi.
The Indian Independence Act of 1947/by Susan Muaddi Darraj.
  p. cm. — (Milestones in modern world history)
Includes bibliographical references and index.
ISBN 978-1-60413-496-4 (hardcover)
1. India—History—Partition, 1947—Juvenile literature. 2. India—Politics and government—20th century—Juvenile literature. 3. Constitutional history—India—Juvenile literature. I. Title. II. Series.

DS480.842.D36 2011
954.03'59—dc22   2011004476

Chelsea House books are available at special discounts when purchased in bulk quantities
for businesses, associations, institutions, or sales promotions. Please call our Special Sales
Department in New York at (212) 967-8800 or (800) 322-8755.

You can find Chelsea House on the World Wide Web at http://www.infobaselearning.com.

Text design by Erik Lindstrom
Cover design by Alicia Post
Composition by Keith Trego
Cover printed by Bang Printing, Brainerd, Minn.
Book printed and bound by Bang Printing, Brainerd, Minn.
Date printed: September 2011
Printed in the United States of America

10 9 8 7 6 5 4 3 2 1

This book is printed on acid-free paper.

All links and Web addresses were checked and verified to be correct at the time of
publication. Because of the dynamic nature of the Web, some addresses and links may
have changed since publication and may no longer be valid.

CONTENTS

The Death of Gandhi

When Mohandas Karamchand Gandhi returned to his native India in 1914, he was hailed as a hero by many of his fellow countrymen. Within a few months, however, these same leaders grew suspicious of the slim, diminutive man who dressed like a peasant and ate nothing but fruit and nuts, even though he was internationally renowned for the work he had done in racially segregated South Africa.

After having attended law school in Great Britain at the age of 19, he practiced law in the African nation and was the first "colored" person to be admitted to the South African bar. While working there, he became agitated by the discriminatory treatment of the Indian population at the hands of the white government. The racism he both witnessed and experienced prompted him to experiment with the philosophy of civil disobedience, which he called satyagraha ("the strength of truth").[1]

While in school in England, he had read the work of American author Henry David Thoreau on civil disobedience and had been inspired by it. In South Africa, he made it a policy to refuse to abide by any law that discriminated against Indians; he protested peacefully, rejecting all forms of violence and opting instead for hunger strikes, imprisonment, sit-ins, and work strikes. Thousands of Indians joined his movement, and eventually they began to win significant legal victories. Gandhi remained in South Africa for 20 years, earning himself a reputation as a champion of the oppressed.

In his native India, which had been suffering under British imperial occupation for almost two centuries, many Indians had taken up the cause of liberation. The leaders of this nationalist movement were largely composed of men from the country's Brahman and other upper castes, most of whom had studied in British-run schools and who spoke English at least as well as their native languages. They felt that while the British Raj, or government, had stifled India in many ways, Indians had also benefited from educational, economic, and techno-logical advances. For example, the Raj had invested millions of pounds in creating a railroad system that crisscrossed over most of the Indian subcontinent, eliminating the days when transportation and travel were arduous tasks.

The view of India's educated, elite nationalist leaders is best expressed by one of Gandhi's mentors, Gopal Krishna Gokhale, who said that "the greatest work of Western education in the present state of India is . . . the liberation of the Indian mind from the thralldom of old-world ideas and the assimilation of all that is highest and best in the life and thought of the West."[2]

Gandhi, however, believed that the British were exploiting India, and that the general population should shun the installa-tion of coal mines, factories, and other industrial trappings. He wanted people to return to their Indian roots and wear Indian-made, traditional clothing (as he himself did), rather than Western-style suits and trousers. He feared that people would

Seen here, Mohandas Gandhi during the early years of his legal practice in Johannesburg, South Africa. Gandhi's experience using civil disobedience to challenge racist laws during the Indian community's struggle for civil rights in South Africa would later influence his work in his native India.

forget their local customs in pursuit of what they considered to be "advanced" Western culture. Thus his fellow countrymen, who had benefited from Western influences and enjoyed their current lifestyles, were disenchanted with him at first, believing him to be a threat to Indian progress.

At the same time, the British Raj believed Gandhi to be a threat to the British Empire. They opened a case file on him when he returned to India in 1914, assembling a collection of facts to determine whether or not he would pose a challenge to their authority. Soon, however, they concluded that the small-framed lawyer was nothing more than an eccentric.

THE FALL

By the spring of 1919, after Gandhi had spent a couple of years touring India and refamiliarizing himself with his native country, he embarked on a mission to bring satyagraha to India. His end goal for India was liberation from the British Raj and self-government, and so he joined the nationalist movement that had already been organizing for several years. But Gandhi broadened its appeal to all Indians, not just for those with education who came from the upper castes.

Satyagraha, which relied on methods of civil disobedience such as work strikes, demonstrations, boycotts of British products, and sit-ins, was not only effective but also agitated the British Raj for several reasons. First, it advocated non-violence, so the military and government had no cause to fear a physical challenge. Second, as historian Denis Judd notes, "satyagraha, practiced on a nationwide scale, promised to involve literally millions of ordinary Indian people in a series of peaceful demonstrations that could eventually undermine the Raj's authority and the British administration's will to rule."[3] In other words, a few Indians who refused to go to work in the mills and coal mines would not have much impact, but thousands doing so at once necessarily caught the attention of the imperial authorities.

Mohandas Gandhi (*center*) is photographed at an evening ashram prayer meeting in India, circa January 1930. His nonviolent civil disobedience campaign helped bring about the end of British rule on the Indian subcontinent.

Also, Gandhi's methods sparked media attention, and news of the events he organized was disseminated throughout the land. Whenever he was jailed, for example (which was often), the story would be placed in the headlines of major newspapers, making other Indians aware of the palpability and strength of the movement to liberate India.

Independence was finally achieved on August 15, 1947, through the Indian Independence Act. But it came at a cost, in the opinion of Gandhi. The act called for the partitioning of the Indian subcontinent into two separate countries: India, which would be the home of the Hindu population, and Pakistan, which would be the home of the Muslim population. The division was due to the fact that Hindu–Muslim tensions had been high for decades. At the time, it seemed the only feasible way that Indians could form a peaceful and effective government.

Gandhi was crushed. The division of India ran counter to all his dreams and hopes for his homeland. He opposed the partitioning of the nation, believing that all of India's diverse subgroups, including Hindus, Muslims, Parsis, Sikhs, and others, could live peacefully together, as they had done for the centuries before the British Raj.

Gandhi's views caused many to turn against him, especially radical Hindus, who believed he was betraying them. Plots to assassinate him were nothing new, but for the first time, Indians themselves were planning these plots. Several attempts were made and failed.

And then one succeeded.

On January 30, 1948, the 78-year-old Gandhi left his home in New Delhi in the evening, on his way to prayer. He was approached by a young Hindu extremist, Nathuram Godse, who called him "*Babuji*," which means "father." Gandhi spoke a few words to him before Godse pulled out a pistol and shot Gandhi three times at point-blank range. As he hit the ground, Gandhi called out "Oh God" several times. He died shortly thereafter.

The partitioning of India had claimed its first victim. There would be many others in the years ahead.

An Ancient Culture

The Indian subcontinent is a land with an ancient culture, dating back some 4,000 years; human life in the region can be traced back much further than that. The name of the country comes from the Indus River (the first civilization on the subcontinent is known as the Indus Valley Civilization, which blossomed from about 3000 B.C. to 1500 B.C.). The Indus River is also the origin of the name of the region's major religion, Hinduism.

Just as rich as its history is India's diversity. Around 1500 B.C., the Aryans, a nomadic tribe that also has roots in Europe and other parts of Asia, invaded northern India and settled there. The Aryans mixed with the Dravidian ethnic tribes that already inhabited the Indus Valley Civilization. The result is what is commonly known as Indian culture, and one of its major outgrowths was Hinduism, or the religion of the people of the Indus region.

There are many different ethnic groups in the country, with several major religions practiced there, including Hinduism, Buddhism, Jainism, Sikhism, Zoroastrianism, Judaism, Christianity, and Islam. In addition, numerous languages are commonly spoken, as well as hundreds of regional dialects. (India has two major linguistic families: Indo-Aryan, which is spoken by almost three-quarters of the population, and Dravidian, which is spoken by about 24 percent of the population.) Therefore, when one wonders what "India" or "Indian culture" comprises, there is not one simple answer.

Furthermore, India is diverse in terms of social class levels. Most countries have (or have had in their history) a simple class division, in which there are nobility and aristocrats at the top, a middle class in between, and a lower class or peasantry where the majority of the population falls. In India, however, a caste system developed through the region's major religion, Hinduism.

In Hinduism, there are four major *varnas*, or classes: the Brahmins (teachers, scholars, and priests), the Kshatriyas (kings and warriors), the Vaishyas (traders), and the Shudras (agriculturists, service providers, and artists). Within each varna, there are a variety of castes. The level of specificity is fascinating, as each caste has its own history and traditions.

There is another class of people, currently known as Dalits, that is comprised of people who are not within the varna system but outside of it. Because of this, they have long been known as the "Untouchables" and have been deliberately excluded from most aspects of society. Throughout India's history, the Dalits have been discriminated against, relegated to the poorest living areas, and allowed to work only in occupations that are considered undesirable.

Within Indian society, the caste system was originally devised as a way to establish order: Each varna and its associated castes occupied one sector of the economy, which was a way to divide labor; members of different castes did not intermarry or, in many cases, inhabit the same villages and towns. Rarely could members of one caste move to another, and when it happened, it usually occurred over several generations.

India's caste system has its problems, which have been criticized by the Indian people themselves. Western historians have always considered the caste system detrimental to India's progress (although many Western nations have also had rigid class systems that denied certain rights to entire populations). Stanley A. Wolpert notes: "India's classic historic weakness has always been rooted in its hierarchical and mutually mistrustful caste system of social fragmentation, undermining cooperation and full use of the potential skills and cumulative power of its diverse peoples."[1]

RELIGIOUS DIVERSITY

India's diversity contributed to the fact that not only Hindus practiced the caste system, even though it originated in that religion. The caste system has been practiced and reinforced in Indian Muslim communities and other societies as well.

Hinduism dates back to approximately 1500 B.C., although there is no one person from whom the religion originates. The general historical view of Hinduism's development is that it came about as the result of the Aryan invasion of the Indus Valley Civilization and the mixing of the Aryan and Dravidian cultures. Just as Hinduism has no single founder (not in the way that Christianity has Jesus of Nazareth and Islam has the prophet Muhammad), it also does not have a centralized core of beliefs. In fact, there are many different forms of Hinduism and ways in which the religion is practiced.

There are, however, some common beliefs to which almost all the sub-sects of Hinduism ascribe. These include the belief in Brahman, one god or supreme being, who has at least three manifestations (Shiva, Vishnu, or Shakti); the belief in reincarnation (that the soul, upon the death of the body, migrates to another body, and that one is not free from this cycle until she or he has achieved enlightenment); and the law of karma (that one's destiny is already predetermined). There are also other lifestyle commonalities—for example, most Hindus do not eat beef, believing that cows are sacred. Of course, as mentioned earlier, the caste system is an outgrowth of the Hindu faith, although some claim that the caste system already existed in the Indus Valley Civilization and simply became incorporated into the Hindu religion as it developed.

Islam, on the other hand, is quite different—in its origins, structure, and belief system. Islam is an outgrowth of Judaism and Christianity; Muhammad, Islam's founder and prophet, was well versed in these other two monotheistic faiths. Muhammad, an orphan who was later employed as a merchant, lived in the Arabian Peninsula between A.D. 570 and 632. He received a series of revelations over several years from God, through the angel Gabriel, and was tasked with spreading the word about Islam. The word *Islam* comes from the Arabic word *salaam*, which means peace; Islam has another meaning, which is "submission," as in submitting to God's will.

Muslims believe in one God (the same God of the Jewish and Christian faiths) and that Muhammad is the last in a long line of prophets sent to reveal God's word. Muslims believe— again in keeping with Islam as the third in a sequence of monotheistic faiths—that Moses, Jesus, and others revered by Jews and Christians were also prophets. They believe that all human beings are children of Adam, the first man, and thus all are equal in status and society. Lifestyle and individual behaviors are also regulated in Islam: Drinking alcohol, gambling, and eating pork are prohibited (the pig is seen as an unclean animal).

While the majority of Indians has always been Hindu, there was a significant minority of Muslims in India before independence. Additionally, there were other religions, such as Jains and Zoroastrians, who also were minorities but were far smaller in number.

CONQUESTS

The invasion of the Indus Valley Civilization by the Aryans was just one of the first-known conquests of the Indian subcontinent. Throughout its history, it has been conquered by various peoples.

One of the more notable conquests was that of the Persian-Muslim Mughals, who brought India into their empire in the late 1600s. Following that invasion, the Persian-Muslim influence became very pronounced in India, so much so that during the era of the Mughal Empire, Muslim culture became an integral part of Hindu culture. Before long, India was a mix of the two.

Prior to that, however, another conquest of India occurred in a subtler, steadier manner. By the late 1500s, British merchants knew that the East Indies was a rich source of trading. They believed that goods found there could be bought and then traded in Europe. A group of merchants formed a company and requested the permission of Queen Elizabeth I to sail to the Indies and investigate the possibility of conducting business there. Shortly thereafter, in 1600, the East India Company of London was granted a royal charter by the British monarch. In 1608, the first of the company's ships began arriving in Indian port cities to purchase goods, spices, and other items to export back to England. A few years later, in 1613, the first permanent British post had been established in India. At that point, P.J. Marshall writes, "a regular direct trade between Britain and India began."[2]

It was not long before the East India Company and its representatives became involved with government as much as with trade. For example, the company's representatives convinced the Mughal emperor to allow it further privileges, specifically the right to a monopoly in India. "John Company," as it was known in England, wanted to rid the market of other competitors, such as the trade-savvy Dutch. Through bribes

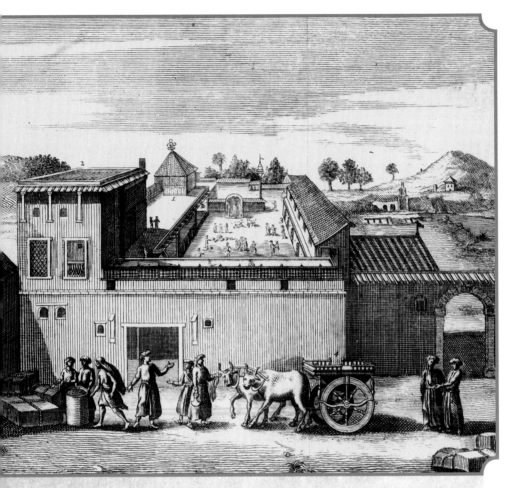

In this circa-1680 illustration, the trading post established by the British East India Company at Surat is shown. Surat, which is also known as Suryapur, is today the commercial capital of the Indian state of Gujarat.

and promises of valuable European goods, the emperor was convinced to grant the East India Company the exclusive right to establish posts in several regions of India. Decades later, the company's three most important posts at Madras, Calcutta, and Bombay, in which members of the company and their families lived, had grown so large that the company's representatives requested—and were granted—by the local rulers and princes the ability to govern themselves.

The company's director, called the governor, oversaw the major workings of the company along with a court of directors, which was comprised of more than 20 members. Before long, the company became quite profitable by trading cotton, silk, tea, and spices—all items that had a high value in England. In 1609, King James I renewed the company's charter. Marshall describes the company's growing power in the following passage: "In a little over fifty years the East India Company was transformed from a body of traders controlling a scattered group of commercial settlements round the coasts of India into the rulers of provinces with a population popularly supposed in Britain to contain fifty or sixty million inhabitants."[3] In reality, the Indian population was much larger and much more diverse than the British assumed.

JOHN COMPANY GROWS

Throughout the 1600s and 1700s, the East India Company expanded both its trading routes and its political power in India. It even had its own army. As it grew, the company experienced problems. In 1757, what is today known as the Battle of Plassey took place. The victory of the company's forces—and its acquisition of the Bengali land and treasury—over the *nawab* (provincial governor or viceroy) of Bengal and his French allies was a decisive historical moment that led to what is called "company rule in India" or "Company Raj," as it was known among Indians.

In the end, the leader of Bengal surrendered the lands he controlled to the company, which now owned actual real estate in India for the first time. In 1772, as its control of land increased, the company established its own capital in the city of Calcutta, where its governor was more than just a company director—he was the leader of a strong collective of British post-cities and ports.

In 1764, the company engaged the army of the Mughal emperor, Shah Alam II, in the Battle of Buxar. After the

Mughal were defeated, they ceded control of Bengal, Bihar, and Orissa to the East India Company. This victory was just as important as the Battle of Plassey because it confirmed the dominance of the company, which now controlled a vast amount of territory in India. The Mughal Empire's era had ended. The Indian subcontinent had been officially conquered and occupied by John Company.

While most of the local rulers generally cooperated with the British company directors, giving in to demands in exchange for certain gifts and loyalties, the local population had grown discontented with the British *sahibs* (which means "masters" or "lords" and was the typical way Indians addressed the Englishmen).

The British considered the Indian population to be of a different race, and many viewed their culture—whether it was Hindu, Muslim, Parsi, Bengali, etc.—to be inferior to that of their own Christian culture. In fact, British missionaries had a long history in India, trying to help people mired in poverty, but also trying to convert them to Christianity, a policy that came to be deeply resented by many Indians. Another issue was exploitation. During its expansion, the company had enhanced many aspects of Indian infrastructure to facilitate its own business dealings. It had also "rescued" many Indians from poverty, in its opinion, by employing them in the business, usually in servant or lower-level jobs: messengers, laborers, soldiers, agricultural workers, household servants, and childcare providers.

From the Indian perspective, however, their nation had been exploited, not improved, and their population had been practically enslaved. One source describes the inequalities: "Beneath the unrelenting sun, Indians toiled for a few farthings a day, under Company and civil-servant employees for whom India was largely the safety-valve for British excess population at home, from younger sons to superfluous daughters."[4] In other words, India was a place for a Briton to come and establish a career, which might otherwise be unlikely in England,

Seen here, Shah Allum Mogul of Hindostan reviews troops of the British East India Company in 1781. Through bribes and persuasion, local Indian princes like the shah effectively gave the East India Company the ability to govern itself.

and to be successful at the expense of the indigenous population. It was a colony where a second son, whose older brother would inherit the family fortune (as per English custom), could sail and make a fortune either in business or in the service of the company's many divisions, or where a family with several daughters could send them to find English husbands. In short, India kept the English economy, society, and culture moving forward, even while—as many Indians viewed it—their own country was moving backward.

Historian Denis Judd notes that the lowest level of Indian society, the large class of peasants and workers, did not seem to care whether they were ruled by a local prince, the Mughal emperor, or the governor-general of the East India Company; they only cared about subsistence and survival. Judd writes that it was the members of the middle and upper castes who were concerned about the company's growing power:

> From the summit of Indian society, however, things could look very different. As a result of the activities of the East India Company, the British had abruptly overthrown Indian rulers, had dispossessed landlords, and had seemed to encourage attacks on the indigenous religious and cultural order.[5]

Because many British had a dismissive and condescending view of the local cultures and traditions, few ever tried to understand those cultures and tried even less to respect them. For example, the British ate beef, which upset Hindus, and they drank alcohol, which upset Muslims. The British posts in Calcutta, Bombay, and elsewhere were not communities of English people living among the Indians, but rather more like groups of Britons replicating their English lifestyles in spite of the local population. This cavalier attitude toward the indigenous populations would have serious repercussions in 1857.

The Indian Mutiny

As previously mentioned, the East India Company had long had its own military, in order to protect its business holdings, its posts, and its employees and employees' families. Small numbers of Indians were allowed to serve in its armies, although those numbers grew steadily during the early 1800s. The Bengal Army was one such regiment. It would become internationally famous in 1857, when its Indian sepoys (the name for Hindu and Muslim members of the military) staged a revolt that led to what is known as the Indian Mutiny, or the Sepoy Mutiny.

The core cause of the mutiny was the insensitivity of the East India Company's military commanders to the traditions of their Indian soldiers. The regiment was being trained to use a new type of gun, the Pattern 1853 Enfield rifle. The rifle featured a greased cartridge; to use it, soldiers had to bite it open

Members of the British Royal Horse Artillery charge against Indian natives near Allahabad, India, during the Sepoy Rebellion of 1857. The revolt, which soon spread to other Indian groups, began when the sepoys felt dishonored by having to take orders from British commanders who had little respect for them.

with their teeth. The problem was that word had spread among the Indian soldiers that the cartridges were being greased with animal fat, specifically from pigs and other animals, possibly cows. Cows are sacred in the Hindu faith, and for Muslims, eating or coming into contact with pigs or pork meat is forbidden.

Before long, sepoys in the Bengal Army refused to use or touch the cartridges. In April 1857, one man was hanged for refusing to use the cartridge, which caused ill will among other soldiers. In May, 85 men in the Bengal Army also refused to use it. They were court-martialed for their refusal to follow orders and some were sentenced to 10 years of hard labor, others to five years in prison—punishments that were considered to be unjust and extremely harsh by their fellow Indian soldiers. To make matters worse, they were paraded in chains and shackles before their comrades as a form of humiliation.

That night, their fellow sepoys attacked the prison to set their comrades free. The men, along with their freed comrades, killed several British officers, as well as some English women and children when they attacked the living quarters of the British soldiers. From Bengal, the Sepoy Mutiny spread to other regions of India, including Uttar Pradesh, Bihar, and Delhi.

Some historians suggest that the greased bullets may not have been the sole cause of the mutiny, which later triggered a wider rebellion. Denis Judd says, "There is, in fact, a good deal of evidence to show that a breakdown in mutual esteem and goodwill had occurred between officers and sepoys well before the great uprising of 1857."[1] Many of the Bengal Army sepoys, who belonged to India's upper castes, felt insulted and demeaned by the rigors of life in the barracks and from having to take orders from British generals who did not respect them or their cultural concerns. Furthermore, the British governor-general of India, Lord Dalhousie, had recently aggravated Indo–British relations by beginning an aggressive policy of annexing Indian land for the company without first consulting with the local rulers, which signaled a break with the company's tradition of working with the princes in order to appeal to the people.

Fueled by the cartridge controversy and these other facts, widespread rebellion spread across many parts of India. The problem with the rebellion was that it was poorly organized and often violent. There was no unified purpose. Some rebels called for the restoration of the Mughal emperor to the throne while others just seemed interested in looting and stealing whatever they could. British newspapers reported incidents in which Indian rebels attacked and ravaged communities of British settlers, such as at Cawnpore (also known as Kanpur).

The Cawnpore incident was a long siege of the British settlement by a group of Indian rebels led by Nana Sahib. The

British had angered Sahib because they refused to pay him a pension, and so his troops attacked the British garrison in the city where the men lived with their wives and children. The outnumbered British sent desperate messages to other generals for help, but the rebels had kept British forces busy elsewhere. The British in Cawnpore, therefore, had to defend themselves as long as possible. For several weeks, Sahib's army tried to break through and overcome the British, who held out for a long time without getting fresh water, food, and other basics. Finally, Sahib offered to transport them to Allahabad if they surrendered; with no other option, they agreed. As the now-unarmed men, women, and children climbed into the boats, they were fired upon by Sahib's troops. It had been a trap. Several women and children managed to escape and make it back to shore, but they were captured and kept in a house called the *Bibighar*, or the "women's house," and made to work during their captivity, grinding cornmeal and doing other chores for Sahib's army.

At some point a few weeks later, Nana Sahib decided to kill those survivors as well. When his rebel troops balked at killing women and children, local butchers were hired to finish the job. The men entered the Bibighar with meat cleavers, killed the prisoners, and dismembered their bodies. The horrific act was then completed when the bodies of the women and children were thrown down a well.

When British reinforcements finally arrived in Cawnpore, the eerie silence told them they were too late. The discovery of the bodies in the well, however, triggered the fury of the British soldiers. The massacre at Cawnpore made headlines of all the British newspapers, even back home in England.

BRITISH VENGEANCE

Many British felt betrayed by a population they believed they had helped. The brutal murders of women and children in

Cawnpore seemed beyond the pale. When the dismembered bodies in the well and the bloodstained walls and floors of the Bibighar house were discovered, the British were determined to teach the rebels a brutal lesson; the military of the East India Company now sought to not only suppress the mutiny but also to exact revenge. Rebels were caught and forced to clean the bloodstains, then killed immediately after. Muslim rebels were covered in pigskin, while Hindu rebels were forced to eat beef before their executions.

The vengeance exacted by the military was extended to innocent civilians, just as the rebels had attacked innocent women and children. Indian villages were burned and destroyed, and many people killed without ever having had a chance to defend themselves or demonstrate that they had not been involved in the original killings. When the mutiny was finally suppressed in 1858, any semblance of trust between the Indian population and the East India Company had been destroyed.

The British population back in England followed the mutiny closely during that year. Daily news stories updated the public on the details of the rebellion and its suppression, each story more horrifying than the last. Judd says, "The Victorian public was gorged on the horrors of the 1857 Indian uprising." Many Britons believed that the mutiny was an attempt to reverse the benefits that the company had brought to the Indian subcontinent, and so, as Judd notes, the British people felt betrayed by the rebellion: "It is not difficult to see why this response [the British feelings of betrayal] took place. The rebellion seemed to be a fundamental reaction against the prevailing Victorian belief in progress."[2]

Indeed, the whole notion of imperialism, as practiced by the British and other European powers in the nineteenth century, held at its core the belief that Western civilization was superior to that of all other cultures. By colonizing these other nations, many Europeans believed they were doing a moral good and helping to spread progress and civilization around the world.

Therefore, the mutiny of 1857–1858 did nothing to correct the views the British held about Indians; the fact that the Indians would rebel and commit atrocities against the very people who were helping to advance India was—as the British viewed it—a clear demonstration of their backwardness and their need for enlightenment. Judd says, "Deep-seated prejudices, which had already been much in evidence before 1857, were confirmed and strengthened. The gulf that had already opened between the two races widened to almost unbridgeable proportions. One of the major casualties was trust."[3]

Another casualty was the East India Company itself.

THE ERA OF THE BRITISH RAJ

The Indian Mutiny, filled with stories about massacres of British women and children by Indian rebels (such as had happened in Cawnpore), caused a major controversy in England. Queen Victoria and her advisers decided that the East India Company could no longer handle its administration of the Indian colony and that the British government needed to assume direct responsibility. In 1858, the Government of India Act was announced. The act effectively replaced the East India Company with the British monarchy as the ruler of India. As Wolpert says, the result was the "transferring 'all rights' that the company had hitherto enjoyed on Indian soil directly to the crown."[4]

The structure of the company administration did not change much; it only was reworked to derive its authority from Queen Victoria rather than from the company's directors. For example, the governor-general was replaced with the viceroy, a representative of the monarchy who was supported by an executive council and who was the final authority on Indian affairs. Furthermore, the monarchy established a position of secretary of state for India; he would have his own advisory

After the East India Company's rule came to an end, the British government established the British Raj—the period of direct British rule that lasted from 1858 to 1947. Seen here, a group of colonials photographed with a pet cheetah at Secunderabad, during the days of the British Raj.

council called the India Council. Although the secretary's position was influential, most of the final decisions pertaining to the colony rested with the viceroy.

Perhaps most importantly, the company's military became part of the British national army and therefore answerable to the British government. Wolpert notes that the refashioned army did have a primary mission: "The company's presidency armies were reorganized as a martially coordinated royal machine designed to prevent any recurrence of rebellion."[5]

More than anything else, the British government and public wanted to avoid another Cawnpore.

Although many facets of the Company Raj remained the same under the British Raj, several changes also occurred. For example, the British government was determined to work with the local rulers and princes to maintain its authority in India. While this had been the policy of the East India Company at

QUEEN VICTORIA, THE EMPRESS OF INDIA

India became known the "Jewel in the Crown" of the British Empire because it was such a valuable colony, providing Great Britain with imports of cotton, tea, and other commodities. Just as the East India Company had profited from it, so would the monarchy after the Government of India Act was passed in 1858. Queen Victoria, who was then the monarch, would become the empress of India.

Born in 1819, Victoria assumed the throne at the age of 18 and reigned for 64 years, until her death in 1901. Her reign, the longest in British history, is remembered mainly for two things: the moral and social influence she cast and the expansion of the British Empire.

Victoria's public image reflected piousness and social conservatism. The family was touted as the central social unit, and women were expected to be obedient wives and devoted mothers. Social decorum was also spotlighted; ladies and gentlemen were expected to wear demure fashions. Even tables were supposed to be covered in long skirts so that the table's legs did not show and thus inadvertently remind someone of a lady's bare legs.

the outset, the company had begun to thwart local rulers as it gained more power over the years. The new officials of the Raj reached out to the local princes to make sure that they had their loyalty, which they requested in exchange for promises of security and other bribes. The number of British soldiers on the subcontinent was also increased, so that the British soldiers serving in India were no longer outnumbered by sepoys. Now that one

After the death of Prince Albert, her husband, in December 1861, Victoria went into a long period of mourning. In the 1870s, she resumed her activities with a more aggressive stance, focusing especially on the issue of the empire. By then, India had been added to the empire, which also included Canada, Australia, large portions of Africa and Asia, and New Zealand. Victoria, guided by her advisers, was an imperialist, determined to bring wealth and prosperity to Britain, as well as to spread Christian values to the regions of the world that she considered uncivilized.

India was her special pride. She "imported" many aspects of Indian culture into her lifestyle at the palace. She served Indian dishes regularly at royal dinners, had at least one room in the palace decorated in Indian fashion, and wore Indian jewelry. She even learned some Hindi, writing letters and diary entries in the language.*

Perhaps what is most revealing about the relationship between India and Britain in that era—what best symbolizes the disconnect between conqueror and conquered—was the fact that Queen Victoria never once visited the land of which she was empress.

* "Passage to India," PBS. http://www.pbs.org/empires/victoria/text/historypassage.html.

company no longer dominated the region, the viceroy also invited other companies to invest in India. Wolpert explains:

> The postwar era proved . . . to be a period of unprecedented European capital investment and commercial agricultural development in British India. Victory convinced private entrepreneurs throughout Britain and Western Europe that the British Empire in India was destined to endure, capable of countering effectively any internal challenge.[6]

One of the most visible results of the investment funds that were pouring into India was the railroad system that was slowly but methodically being built. While the railroads were initially intended to help transport goods and supplies, their growth and development benefited the local population as well. For the first time, for example, Indians in the northern regions could travel, relatively quickly and safely, to the south, east, west, or central regions.

Another change was the establishment of the Indian Civil Service (ICS). The East India Company had previously established a similar organization, but now it was expanded and revamped by the monarchy. The ICS included almost 1,500 officials who made up the overall administration of the colony of India, including governing cities, a postal service, medical services, transportation, courts, and other facets.

The Rise of
the Resistance

The official establishment of India as a British colony did not really change life for the average Indian: The occupiers were still British and still foreign, but now they just belonged to a national government rather than to a company. Life even improved in some ways, because more jobs were available in industry, since the railroad system was being built, and in the Indian Civil Service, which was more open to native Indians as the decades passed.

What did not improve was the prevailing British attitude toward the Indian population. Prejudice was deep-rooted and pervasive, and the mutiny of 1857–1858 had allowed the hatred and distrust to become more visible. Many Indians realized that, under the Raj, their country would always belong to another nation. They also deeply resented the way in which their country was belittled and their traditional practices suppressed.

For example, one custom that caused strife between the British and the Indians was *sati*, the practice of widow burning. (In the Hindu faith, Sati was the name of a goddess, the wife of the god Shiva, who committed suicide by setting herself on fire.) In sati, the recently widowed wife of a man would throw herself onto the funeral pyre, killing herself in order to join her husband in death and be reunited with him in the afterlife. Self-immolation was regarded as the ultimate symbol of one's grief, and so the widow who committed sati was respected as an upright, decent, chaste woman. While the practice was not prevalent in all of India (in some regions, it was looked upon with horror), in places where it was customary, it had a long history, dating back to before the tenth century.

During the time of the Company Raj, the British realized that this tradition—which was originally linked with the Kshatriyas, or the warrior caste, but had spread to other castes as well—was widespread in India. In 1829, the Company Raj, under Governor-General William Bentinck, outlawed the practice of sati. In contemplating the ban, knowing it would arouse anger among some Indians, Bentinck finally concluded: "I should be guilty of little short of the crime of multiplied murder if I could hesitate in the performance of this solemn obligation. . . . Every day's delay adds a victim to the dreadful list."[1] The reason for the ban was not just the shock and horror the British felt about the practice, but reports that many of the widows were forced to their deaths—either by being pushed into the fire, drugged, or tied onto the pyre. Why were so many widows forced to their deaths? Families, for reasons of honor, wanted to show that the widows were completely devoted to their husbands; other widows were murdered because they would have become financial burdens on either their own or their husbands' families. Thus, the ritual suicide was often not suicide at all, but murder. Despite this, for many Hindus, the ban on sati was seen as foreign interference with their traditions and culture.

Thus, after the Crown Raj was established and after it continued to uphold certain bans, such as the one on sati, many Indian communities, both Hindu and Muslim, began to see things in terms of "foreign" versus "traditional." Denis Judd writes:

> One of the unexpected results of the crushing of the rebellion was the strengthening of conservatism within the subcontinent; as a result, orthodox Hinduism experienced a revival. Prior to 1857 reformist elements had been in the ascendant, but subsequent reaction tended to promote and sanctify the more obscure and traditionalist qualities of Hinduism as a protection against the inroads of "corrupting" and "dangerous" British ideas and influence.[2]

Although Hinduism does not have a single sacred text or even a code or creed of beliefs, those Hindus who felt that the British Raj had lasted long enough needed an organizing principle; they used their religion to assemble themselves into a single group calling for freedom. Their message—Indian nationalism—became mixed with their religion, so much so that they even called for an independent India for Hindus only. In mixing their political views with their religious ones, they rejected anything that was European and embraced Hindu cultural and religious practices. Many Hindus began to adhere to a more traditional interpretation of Hinduism and adopted a pro-Hindu, anti-British political viewpoint.

Around this time, Muslims in India were undergoing a transformation in their own community. In light of the British occupation and the crackdown on Hindu culture, Muslims looked to their own religion and culture to solidify their identities. There was also a call for a return to authentic Muslim values as a way to protect them from what they believed were the corrupting Western values of the British.

Unfortunately, Muslims and Hindus in India—both of whom felt threatened by the British influence—did not organize themselves around their common identity of being Indian. They were more selective and specific, retreating within their own communities rather than making connections with others who had similar concerns about the British. This division, an exacerbation of previous tensions between the groups, would have violent consequences for the nation.

THE RISE OF INDIAN NATIONALISM

Indian nationalism—the political movement aimed at liberating India from British rule—took many forms in the late nineteenth century, with several nationalist organizations cropping up in the 1870s and 1880s. Ironically, but not surprisingly, the earliest nationalist leaders were mostly men who had received an English education and admired British culture. Their ideas of "nationalism" and "resistance" took a political form learned from the English themselves: to organize politically.

The first Indian organization with a nationalist agenda focused on the liberation of India was the Indian Association, formed in 1876, by Surendranath Banerjea. Other organizations included the Congress Party, which formed in 1885 and consisted mainly of Hindu members who had a secular agenda, and the Muslim League, which formed in 1906 and aimed to be the unified voice of Indian Muslims. Many of its members felt that the Congress Party was too heavily Hindu in its makeup and influence.

It can be said that Indian nationalism truly began to emerge in 1885, three decades after the Indian Mutiny and the establishment of the British Raj. At this point, the fact that India was now officially a British colony was unacceptable to many Indians. Wolpert writes, "All Indians, whatever their religious, caste, or regional origins may have been, were immediately conscious of the 'foreign' character of the white Christian *sahibs* who ruled their land, if they had any direct contact with these new rulers at all."[3]

THE CONGRESS PARTY

The Indian National Congress, later known as the Congress Party, was the first Indian nationalist party to have widespread support and political clout. Its founders included Mahadev Govind Ranade, a lawyer, and Gopal Krishna Gokhale, an advocate for education. Because of his education and training in the law, Ranade knew how the British justice system worked and attacked the problem of the British occupation like a court case. Wolpert writes:

> Ranade sought to help his countrymen win their freedom by making full and effective use of all the political institutions and self-governing ideals embodied in British society and English literature and law. He always armed himself with facts and drafted his appeals for social, economic, and political reform with the brilliance and persuasive force of the great legal mind he was.[4]

Gokhale was a student of Ranade and followed his mentor's political lead; Wolpert calls Gokhale "Ranade's foremost disciple."[5] Gokhale supported a strong educational system as a way to help modernize India and make its people more informed and invested in the future of the country. As Wolpert points out, Ranade and Gokhale believed that India would never be liberated unless Indians modernized their ways: "The Ranade-Gokhale school of nationalism also insisted upon the need for Indians to reform their own social and religious ideas and resolve internal conflicts as a prerequisite to political independence."[6] Another important leader of the Congress Party was Motilal Nehru, a wealthy lawyer and local politician, who twice served as its president.

Several aspects of Indian culture needed modernization, including the treatment of women, the Indian educational system, and the elimination of the caste system to end the

In this circa-1899 photo, the future Indian statesman Jawaharlal Nehru sits for a photograph with his father, Motilal Nehru, and mother, Swarup Rani Nehru. Motilal Nehru was a leading early Indian independence activist.

discrimination and class hatred it promoted. Some of the Congress Party's priorities included gaining equal rights for Indians under the Raj (such as by allowing more Indians to be part of the Indian Civil Service) and better education and employment opportunities for Indians. They also sought to have more Indian representation on important councils and government bodies.

When the Congress's first meeting took place in 1885, it consisted mostly of educated and middle- and upper-class Hindus. While some members of other religions, including Islam, were present, they were not well represented. The Congress also did not represent most of the lower castes. Nevertheless, the Congress believed that, as members of India's more educated and politically savvy segment, they were better suited to lead the nationalist movement; one Congress leader said that the members of Congress were the "true interpreters and mediators between the masses of our countrymen and our rulers."[7]

THE MUSLIM LEAGUE

In 1905, the British Raj's viceroy made a controversial decision. The Bengal region was becoming overpopulated at 85 million people and too large and unwieldy for the ICS to administer. The viceroy thus concluded that it would be best to divide the land into two separate regions.

The problem was this: The Bengali people, who were Hindu, were the ethnic majority in the Bengal region. Dividing it along the lines proposed by the viceroy would lead to a western Bengal, in which the majority were other ethnic groups who did not speak Bengali, and an eastern Bengal, in which the majority were Muslim, not Hindu. In other words, splitting the Bengal region also divided the Bengali people, erasing the power of their majority and instead making them the minority in two separate regions. Indians, seeing this as another example of the British lack of regard for Indian opinion and sentiment, angrily protested the move. Gokhale, one of the Congress's founders and most vocal leaders, said:

> A cruel wrong has been inflicted on our Bengalee [sic] brethren . . . and the whole country has been stirred to its deepest depths in sorrow and resentment, as had never been the

MUHAMMAD ALI JINNAH

Muhammad Ali Jinnah, along with Jawaharlal Nehru, Mohandas Gandhi, and Lord Mountbatten, was one of the key figures in the independence of India.

Born in 1876, Jinnah was part of a prosperous Shiite Muslim family in what is now Karachi, Pakistan, but was then India. Although he became the leader of India's Muslim community, Jinnah was not an observant Muslim. He had, like many of the other early nationalist leaders, benefited from Western culture and education and enjoyed wearing Western clothing and speaking and reading English. His role model was Gopal Krishna Gokhale, whom he strove to emulate, even saying that he wanted to be the "Muslim Gokhale."

He studied law in both Bombay and London (where he met and befriended Mohandas Gandhi) and established a successful law practice in India. A nationalist, he joined the Indian National Congress and became one of its most important voices on the unity of the Hindu and Muslim communities—the two groups needed to work together, he believed, in order to attain Indian liberation.

When he learned of the formation of the Muslim League, he joined in 1913. Three years later, in 1916, he became its president, continuing to work toward unity, to suppress the tension that already existed between the two case before. The scheme of partition, concocted in the dark and carried out in the face of the fiercest opposition that any Government measure has encountered during the last half-a-century, will always stand as a complete illustration of the worst features of the present system of bureaucratic rule—its utter contempt for public opinion, its arrogant pretentions to

communities, and to strengthen their common agenda of freedom. As president, he helped steward the Lucknow Pact, a formal agreement between Hindu and Muslims to work together toward their goal of liberation.

Years later, however, he grew to feel that the Indian National Congress had become a party that sought a liberated India that was Hindu in character, and that there would be little room for the Muslim population. Much of this sentiment arose from the fact that Gandhi had become associated with the Congress Party, and the mahatma's style of liberation was deeply spiritual and Hindu in nature. Jinnah saw this as divisive, even though Gandhi himself called for Hindu-Muslim unity. In 1920, Jinnah officially left the Congress and devoted himself to the Muslim League, although he became disillusioned by the party's internal politics. He left India for England to practice law but was persuaded to return in 1934 when the Muslim League, newly reunited, called upon him to resume his leadership.

Jinnah was still optimistic that Muslims and Hindus could work together, despite their differences. After 1937, when the popular Congress rejected his call that the two parties work together and share power, Jinnah adopted the idea of a separate nation for the Muslim population to be carved out of the Indian colony. This new nation, Pakistan, was born when India became independent, and Jinnah served as its first governor-general.

superior wisdom, its reckless disregard of the most cherished feelings of the people, the mockery of an appeal to its sense of justice, its cool preference of Service interests to those of the governed.[8]

The protests sparked by the division of the Bengal region were fierce. Indians felt that the British had gone too far in trying to change the demographics of India and in manipulating the populations that it felt had too much power.

As previously mentioned, other groups began to organize during this time too, especially Muslim Indians, many of whom felt that the Congress Party served only Hindu interests. Wolpert writes, "India's largest minority community never really came to feel 'at home' inside Congress."[9] As a result, the Muslim League was formed in 1906. It initially enjoyed recognition by the British Raj, which is not surprising. Many English officials felt that they could "divide and conquer" the nationalist movement by pitting the Hindus and the Muslims against each other. Wolpert writes, "India's Muslims, like its landlords and princes, were viewed as blocs of potential support for the new Crown Raj, especially after the seas of nationalism began to swell and rise."[10]

The Muslim League's political views were influenced by men like Sayyid Ahmad Khan, a Muslim scholar and founder of the Anglo-Mohammedan Oriental College in India. Khan's family had close ties with the former Mughal emperor, and he himself had good relations with the British, having been employed by the East India Company as a young man. After the Indian Mutiny, however, he published a widely read essay, "The Causes of the Indian Revolt," in which he criticized the British administration of India. Though he believed in Indian modernization, he did not agree with the Congress Party's insistence on independence; he thought India would prosper best under the Raj. Furthermore, he believed that an independent India with an elected government was a poor idea, claiming that the government would become dominated by those who had a high level of education, which was unfair.

Though he had initially supported Hindu–Muslim cooperation, Khan eventually advised Muslims not to join the Congress Party. He insisted that good relations with the British were important for the success of the Muslim population in India. Wolpert says that Khan became "India's first human bridge between Islamic tradition and Western thought."[11] Khan had grown wary of the Hindu brand of nationalism that, he feared, would drown out the voice of the Muslims in India. For example, he was particularly alarmed by some local movements to eliminate the Urdu language (which Muslims in northern India spoke) and replace it with Hindi. When the Muslim League was formed, he supported it as a way to make sure that the Muslim voice was not suppressed.

In 1916, the Muslim League selected Muhammad Ali Jinnah, an English-educated lawyer, as its president. Jinnah would become the most influential leader of the League, advocating for cooperation with Hindus, although he would eventually call for a division of Muslims and Hindus into separate states.

Two years earlier, Mohandas Gandhi had returned to India and had begun to be active in the nationalist movement. Though Gandhi himself called for unity among Indians, Hindu–Muslim tensions were exacerbated because he brought a Hindu influence to the activities of Congress. Influenced by the example of Gandhi and his satyagraha movement, the Indian National Congress launched a movement of civil disobedience and noncooperation in 1920; their official policy was not to adhere to any aspects of British law or rule. The Muslim League, led by Jinnah, opposed this policy; early on in the nationalist movement, Jinnah and Indian Muslims thought it best that India have limited self-government but remain under the wing of the British Empire.

Calls for
Independence

In 1919, a controversy erupted that provided Gandhi with his chance to launch his campaign of nonviolent resistance.

That year, the Raj passed the Rowlatt Acts as a way to counter the rising forces of Indian nationalism. This series of laws, so named because it had been recommended by a commission chaired by Sir Sidney Rowlatt, gave the Raj the authority to imprison any individual or group of individuals suspected of revolutionary activity without the burden of proving their guilt. The laws in effect cracked down on civil liberties such as the right to organize, assemble, and speak freely; they also suppressed freedom of the press.

The acts were technically an extension of the Defense of India Act, which had been passed in 1915 while Britain was engaged in World War I (1914–1918). The Defense of India

Act gave the Raj emergency war powers over the Indian people, suspending many of their civil and political rights. Whatever the reasoning behind the act, Indians were outraged that, once the war ended, those emergency powers remained in place. Indians were particularly upset because they had willfully supported the British during the war—thousands of Indians had even served and died in the British military. (Interestingly, the Raj had been relieved at this generally cooperative attitude among Indians, having assumed that Indians would not cooperate and that British authorities could face mutiny in their prime colony in addition to a war in Europe.)

Mohandas Gandhi saw the brewing outrage over the Rowlatt Acts as a perfect opportunity to introduce his concept of satyagraha to the Indian nationalist movement. As he wrote:

> When the Rowlatt Bills were published I felt that they were so restrictive of human liberty that they must be resisted to the utmost. I observed too that the opposition to them was universal among Indians. I submit that no State however despotic has the right to enact laws which are repugnant to the whole body of the people, much less a Government guided by constitutional usage and precedent such as the Indian Government. I felt too that the oncoming agitation needed a definite direction if it was neither to collapse nor to run into violent channels. I ventured therefore to present Satyagraha to the country emphasizing its civil-resistance aspect.[1]

The Congress Party endorsed Gandhi's beliefs and called for nonviolent resistance to the passage of the acts. In turn, Gandhi organized a *hartal*, or a work strike, on April 6, in which Indians refused to work or conduct business and instead fasted as a sign of their rejection of the Rowlatt Acts. Around the same time, in response to the British crackdown and imprisonment of several political activists and resistance leaders, a major protest, peaceful in nature, began to gather in the Jallianwala Bagh area of the city of Amritsar in northern India. Inspired and galvanized by how the hartal had shaken

SATYAGRAHA AND MOHANDAS GANDHI

Mohandas Gandhi was a prolific writer as well as a lawyer and activist. In the following excerpt from his book *Non-Violent Resistance (Satyagraha)*, he defines satyagraha and the powerful way that it can counter social and political injustice:

> For the past thirty years I have been preaching and practicing Satyagraha. The principles of Satyagraha, as I know it today, constitute a gradual evolution.
>
> Satyagraha differs from Passive Resistance as the North Pole from the South. The latter has been conceived as a weapon of the weak and does not exclude the use of physical force or violence for the purpose of gaining one's end, whereas the former has been conceived as a weapon of the strongest and excludes the use of violence in any shape or form.
>
> The term *Satyagraha* was coined by me in South Africa to express the force that the Indians there used for full eight years and it was coined in order to distinguish it from the movement then going on in the United Kingdom and South Africa under the name of Passive Resistance.
>
> Its root meaning is holding on to truth, hence truthforce. I have also called it Love-force or Soul-force. In the application of Satyagraha I discovered in the earliest stages that pursuit of truth did not admit of violence being inflicted on one's opponent but that he must be weaned

the local administration, thousands of Indians gathered to demand the release of some Congress Party leaders who had been detained without a trial.

from error by patience and sympathy. For what appears to be truth to the one may appear to be error to the other. And patience means self-suffering. So the doctrine came to mean vindication of truth not by infliction of suffering on the opponent but on one's self.

But on the political field the struggle on behalf of the people mostly consists in opposing error in the shape of unjust laws. When you have failed to bring the error home to the lawgiver by way of petitions and the like, the only remedy open to you, if you do not wish to submit to error, is to compel him by physical force to yield to you or by suffering in your own person by inviting the penalty for the breach of the law. Hence Satyagraha largely appears to the public as Civil Disobedience or Civil Resistance. It is civil in the sense that it is not criminal.

The lawbreaker breaks the law surreptitiously and tries to avoid the penalty, not so the civil resister. He ever obeys the laws of the State to which he belongs, not out of fear of the sanctions but because he considers them to be good for the welfare of society. But there come occasions, generally rare, when he considers certain laws to be so unjust as to render obedience to them a dishonour. He then openly and civilly breaks them and quietly suffers the penalty for their breach. And in order to register his protest against the action of the law givers, it is open to him to withdraw his co-operation from the State by disobeying such other laws whose breach does not involve moral turpitude.*

* M.K. Gandhi, *Non-Violent Resistance (Satyagraha)*. New York: Schocken Books, 1961, pp. 6-7.

The local British military leaders were nervous, perhaps fearing another uprising like the 1857 mutiny. It is possible they were also made nervous by the riots, burnings, and attacks that had taken place in the last several days in other parts of India; some British soldiers and civilians had been killed and government property had been destroyed. As strikes continued, the Raj was especially concerned about the several thousand Indians who worked for the railway system, as their work strike hurt the administration's abilities to control their regions and transport troops and supplies.

Whatever their reasons, the Raj's military forces acted hastily and irrationally in response to the hartal. The local governor, Michael O'Dwyer, and Brigadier-General Reginald Dyer, whose army unit arrived at the Jallianwala Bagh to contain the protests, allegedly agreed that it would be appropriate to fire into the crowds. Dyer's forces fired well more than 1,000 rounds of ammunition. (O'Dwyer himself was, several years later, assassinated by a Punjabi nationalist for his role in the Raj's violent response.) According to India's *Frontline* magazine, the scene was chaotic:

> A few minutes before sunset, the first of 1,650 rounds were fired into the crowd. Congress leader Durga Das at first believed the shots were fired into the air, but soon realised bodies were falling all around him. No warning was given to disperse before Dyer opened fire. Many died when they jumped into the well at the left-hand side of the maidan, only to be crushed by others who desperately dived on top of them. The wounded cried for help, but there was no aid at hand.[2]

The number of people who were killed that day remains in dispute. Some historians place it around 300, while others at 1,000 or more. What is certain, however, is that the Amritsar Massacre (also known as the Jallianwala Bagh Massacre) was one of the bloodiest episodes in India's journey toward inde-

At the Amritsar Massacre, British troops commanded by Brigadier-General Reginald Dyer suppressed an illegal demonstration by firing into an unarmed crowd. Historians believe between 300 and 1,000 people were killed on that day in April 1919.

pendence, as well as one of the major events that galvanized the nationalist movement. Brigadier-General Dyer was later found guilty by a British inquiry commission of not warning the demonstrators to disperse before firing, although he was not punished. This mere rebuke of the man who had ordered the massacre outraged Indians even further, cementing the belief among many that the British cared little about Indian life and dignity.

In the nationalist movement's early years, many had believed that India could remain under the Raj as long as Indians had more liberties and equal treatment. After the Amritsar Massacre, however, more and more Indians began talking about being fully liberated from the Raj's oppression.

PATHS TOWARD INDEPENDENCE

Without a doubt, Mohandas Gandhi and his grassroots, action-oriented movement was making the British administration nervous. With one call—for a hunger strike, for a work strike, for the assembly of a peaceful protest—Gandhi could galvanize millions of Indians. While many members of the Congress Party adopted his views (such as the young Jawaharlal Nehru), still others thought that the way forward was through constitutional law. Furthermore, many Muslims had joined the Muslim League by now, feeling that Gandhi's spiritual approach and his affiliation with Congress did not leave room for their voices.

Another aspect of Gandhi's movement was his insistence that Indians return to their customs and traditions; he encouraged his followers to wear their own traditional homespun clothing rather than Western attire, for example. He also wanted people to use their Indian-made commodities and products and to boycott British products. In 1930, he led a successful satyagraha in response to a British tax on salt; the protest took the form of a march to the seacoast near the village of Dandi to make their own salt.

During these years after World War I, the British realized that they would have to allow some level of self-rule for the Indians, which they hoped to achieve while still maintaining their authority over the country. To facilitate that, the Government of India Act was passed in 1919. It provided more opportunities for Indians to participate in the governing of India and also authorized the establishment of a commission that would create some much-needed political reforms for India. Headed by Sir John Simon, the commission and its all-British members began their work several years later. The British composition of the Simon Commission, as it was called, angered the Indians.

In response, Indian nationalist leaders decided to create their own constitutional framework for a future Indian state.

Mohandas Gandhi (*shirtless*) is photographed walking with supporters during the Salt March, conducted on March 12, 1930. A campaign of non-violent protest against the British salt monopoly in colonial India, it helped to trigger the wider civil disobedience movement on the subcontinent.

The challenge was taken seriously by those leaders, like Motilal Nehru, who believed in a constitutional approach to the problem. In 1928, a series of pan-Indian conferences, attended by all nationalist political parties, was held to discuss the various issues. One of the main questions they deliberated was whether it was in India's best interest to seek complete independence or to remain within the British Empire with dominion status, as was the case with Australia and Canada. Furthermore, how would India's self-government be shaped, given its various ethnic and religious constituencies?

The decision was made to form a small commission to draft a framework for Indian self-governance. Composed mostly of Hindus (there were two Muslims on it), the commission was chaired by Motilal Nehru. The Nehru Commission's recommendations disappointed many members of the Muslim

JAWAHARLAL NEHRU

Born in 1889 to a wealthy political family (his father was Motilal Nehru, who twice served as president of the Congress Party), Jawaharlal Nehru was the Hindu counterpart to Muslim leader Muhammad Ali Jinnah. The Nehrus were Brahmin (members of the priestly class of the subcontinent) who hailed from the region of Kashmir in northern India. Growing up in his father's mansion, Jawaharlal and his two sisters were taught to read and speak Hindi, Sanskrit, and English. As their father was a great admirer of Western customs and dress, so the children were raised in the same way.

Jawaharlal, whose name means "red jewel," was the Nehrus' only son. He was educated at the finest schools in England, spending seven years in London attaining a law degree. He returned to India in 1912 and became active in politics a few years later. His political perspective on India's liberation differed from that of his father, having been shaped by Mohandas Gandhi, who became one of the most important influences on young Jawaharlal. Gandhi advocated rejecting Western ways and embracing Indian traditions (even Motilal, who admired Western traditions, was eventually won over to Gandhi's views and gave up his Western lifestyle), as well as a grassroots civil disobedience movement to oust the British from India.

League, who felt that one recommendation, establishing Hindi as the official language, was exclusive enough, but that another, forbidding separate electorates for minorities, was especially distressing. Muslims had always called for the provision of separate electorates, hoping that it would help preserve the Muslim

Nehru became influential in the Congress Party and assumed the presidency after his father. An active leader in Gandhi's Quit India movement and satyagraha resistance to British rule, he was imprisoned several times. In fact, he spent approximately nine years of his life in jail, where, incidentally, he spent much of his time writing. He even composed a series of letters to his daughter and only child, Indira, in which he attempted to relate to her all the things he wished he could have taught her himself, were they not separated. The resulting letters were later published as *Letters from a Father to his Daughter* and *Glimpses of World History: Being Further Letters to His Daughter, Written in Prison and Containing a Rambling Account of History for Young People*.

As head of the Congress and as second-in-command to Gandhi, Nehru was also a lead negotiator in the plans that eventually led to the independence of India and the separation of India and Pakistan. He was named India's first prime minister, a post he held until his death in 1964.

As prime minister, he focused on modernizing the Indian nation as well as handling the aftermath of the separation from Pakistan. His daughter, Indira, became prime minister of India herself, elected twice to the position; she was assassinated in 1984 and succeeded by her son Rajiv Gandhi, who was assassinated in 1991. His son, Rahul Gandhi, the great-grandson of Jawaharlal Nehru, became a member of the Indian parliament in 2004.

voice and maintain Muslim representation in government. To do away with it made it clear to Jinnah and other Muslim leaders that their future was not secure in a Hindu-controlled India.

The Nehru Report met with widespread disfavor. Not only was it rejected by most Muslims, but also by many Hindus who wanted a totally liberated India, not a country that was a self-governed dominion of Britain, as the Nehru Report recommended. Therefore, while the Congress Party, which had the support of many Indians, endorsed the report, it was not at all satisfactory to all Indians.

In January 1930, the Congress declared that it would fight for *Purna Swaraj*, which meant complete self-rule and independence from the British Empire. With its new president, Jawaharlal Nehru, in place, the Congress issued a Declaration of Independence from the British Empire:

> We believe that it is the inalienable right of the Indian people, as of any other people, to have freedom and to enjoy the fruits of their toil and have the necessities of life, so that they may have full opportunities of growth. We believe also that if any government deprives a people of these rights and oppresses them the people have a further right to alter it or to abolish it. The British government in India has not only deprived the Indian people of their freedom but has based itself on the exploitation of the masses, and has ruined India economically, politically, culturally, and spiritually. We believe therefore, that India must sever the British connection and attain *Purna Swaraj* or complete independence.[3]

Not all, however, were content with the declaration. Muhammad Ali Jinnah did not want a complete break from the British Empire because he believed that a connection to the British could help preserve the Muslim voice in a Hindu majority. The Muslim League, led by Jinnah, had now begun to consider that the future of Muslims lay not in a future Indian state, but in a nation of their own.

THE IDEA OF PARTITION

In 1935, the British Parliament passed another Government of India Act (a number of acts bore this title). Judd notes that its passage "seemed virtually to guarantee India independence in the near future. Under the new constitution, although the Raj still kept control of central government, in the 11 provinces power was handed over to elected legislative assemblies and the executive councils that derived from them."[4]

With this act's passage, Indians began to prepare for some sort of self-government. Provincial elections, held for the first time in 1937, yielded big wins for the Congress Party, which had grown more popular because of Gandhi's successful satyagraha. The Muslim League had not done particularly well; in fact, the Congress Party had made gains in areas with large Muslim populations as well. Jinnah reached out to Congress leaders to form coalition administrations with the League in areas with mixed Hindu–Muslim populations, but he was rebuffed.

Jinnah was angered by the rebuff, and the Muslim League grew worried. Independence or self-government of some sort was imminent, and it seemed like the Congress Party would lead the new nation. How would Muslims fare in a new environment dominated by Hindus, without British protection? As Judd says, "Many of India's Muslims became alarmed at the prospect of the British Raj being replaced by what they feared would turn out to be a Hindu Raj."[5]

From 1939 to 1945, Great Britain fought the Second World War. The effort to fight the Axis powers of Germany, Italy, and Japan all but exhausted its military and economy. Maintaining a world-spanning empire began to seem more like a burden than a profitable endeavor. In the postwar years, it became clear to most Britons and Indians that at some point in the near future, Great Britain would turn over control of India to its people. Whether it would be completely or in some kind of dominion status, as the Nehru Report recommended, was the question. In these years before independence, the great empire tried to find an answer, often starting down one path only to change directions.

In 1940, due to the disappointment of the 1937 elections and the refusal of Congress to form a coalition government, the Muslim League for the first time demanded that India be partitioned. Partition meant that a Muslim state—Pakistan—would be carved out of the Muslim regions of the Indian sub-continent. Jinnah was not happy about this demand but felt that the Muslim League had no alternative. The BBC writes: "Jinnah had always believed that Hindu–Muslim unity was possible, but reluctantly came to the view that partition was necessary to safeguard the rights of Indian Muslims."[6] In his view, the growing radicalism of some segments of the Hindu population, the popularity of Gandhi and his Hindu-minded approach to freedom, and the Hindu majority in the Congress Party made it clear that the Muslim minority would be disadvantaged in India.

The Raj was crumbling, and India's future was uncertain. India might gain independence after so long, but what would such independence look like?

Independence
at Last

Despite its victory alongside the Allied powers of the United States and the Soviet Union, Great Britain paid a terrible price during World War II. The German blitzkrieg on the British Isles had destroyed much of the country's infrastructure and nearly 500,000 British citizens had been killed in the war.

The general election of 1945 brought the Labour Party to power in the British Parliament. The Labour Party, led by Clement Attlee, was more liberal than the previous government of Prime Minister Winston Churchill's Conservative Party. Attlee knew he had to get the nation back on its feet after the devastating effects of the war. In order to do so, he and the Labour Party created the National Health Service and other social services to help the country begin to repair itself.

Attlee, who had served as deputy prime minister under Churchill during the war, had long supported granting India its independence. The "jewel in the crown" of Great Britain had been in turmoil for so long, and it was clear from the ongoing nationalist movement and the persistent political wrangling that it would be in England's best interests to leave. The British members of the Indian Civil Service and the military stationed in India were growing disillusioned by the crumbling colony. The renowned author George Orwell, who had served in India, had written: "All over India there are Englishmen who secretly loathe the system of which they are part."[1]

Perhaps the only thing that united India's two warring political parties—the Congress Party and the Muslim League— was their sense of frustration with the British government and its inability to negotiate a clear, clean withdrawal. As one Congress member said, "Nobody worships the setting sun."[2]

Now that Attlee was prime minister, the dream of Indian independence began to seem possible. In fact, during the two years between 1945 and independence in 1947, things moved rapidly and surprisingly toward that goal.

CALCUTTA MASSACRE

In 1946, Attlee sent a three-member mission to India to try to put a specific plan into place for Indian independence. The mission met with members of the Constituent Assembly of India, and in May 1946, the mission declared that it had drafted a plan for an Indian nation that would have dominion status and would be self-governed but remain part of the British Commonwealth. A month later, Jinnah used his influence to convince the mission to put out an alternate plan, one for two dominions: India and Pakistan. For several years now, the Muslim League had come to believe that partition was the only way to secure Muslim rights and security.

The Congress Party immediately rejected the second plan. Jawaharlal Nehru, angered by the notion of partition, renewed a call for a united, independent India. He knew that Congress, as the nation's largest political party, enjoyed strong support among the Indian people, but he also worried that Jinnah would influence the British. In the 1945–1946 elections, the Muslim League had made gains, dominating the Muslim-majority territories in the votes they earned. Jinnah could—and would—use this as a way to push for the goals of the Muslim League during negotiations. Judd writes, "Jinnah's claim that the Muslim League was the true, indeed the only, voice of Islam in India seemed to have sufficiently firm foundations."[3]

Jinnah used the weapon he had—the mostly unified voice of the Muslims of India—and resorted to pressure. Emphasizing the fact that Muslims had always been in the minority in a country with a Hindu majority, he said: "We have exhausted all reason. . . . There is no tribunal to which we can go. The only tribunal is the Muslim Nation."[4]

Declaring August 16, 1946, as "Direct Action Day," he called upon the nation's Muslims to demonstrate in support of the separate state of Pakistan to be carved out of India. General strikes would be called as well. The demonstrations would take place in several cities that had large Muslim populations, such as the city of Calcutta in the province of Bengal, one of India's largest urban areas.

The idea of a separate state being carved out of India infuriated many Hindus, who wanted to preserve India's boundaries. Many of Calcutta's Hindus grew angry as plans for Direct Action Day were put into place. During the month between Jinnah's announcement in July and the actual date of the campaign, resentment and anger brewed. On the day itself, it did not take long for violence to break out between Muslim demonstrators and nationalist Hindus. The riots lasted several days. People were dragged from their homes and slaughtered in the streets, shops and businesses were attacked, and homes were looted and burned. The savagery continued until 15,000 people lay dead in the streets of Calcutta and more than 10,000 people had been left homeless. It is not known whether more Hindus or Muslims were killed, but it is clear that both sides suffered tremendous casualties.

The Calcutta massacre, or Calcutta riots, stunned Indians and British alike—it seemed that a civil war had broken out. The violence spread like a virus. More riots broke out after the Calcutta massacres in other parts of India that had Hindu–Muslim mixed populations. Gandhi felt heartbroken by the divisiveness and hatred and called for peace and understanding. He began to preach Hindu–Muslim unity more aggressively, even reciting verses from the Islamic holy book, the Koran, at his prayer services. Rather than encourage unity, however, his actions only turned some radical Hindus against him. As Wolpert notes, some Hindus even began referring to the respected peace activist as "Muhammad Gandhi" and "Jinnah's slave."[5]

Despite Gandhi's efforts and the efforts of leaders like him, the fury that had been allowed to spill over in Calcutta could not be contained. The British realized that they had reached a point of no return. They had to leave India as quickly and efficiently as possible.

NEGOTIATIONS AND A RESOLUTION

On February 20, 1947, Prime Minister Attlee announced, according to Rajni Kothari, that "his government had decided to transfer power into Indian hands at the latest by June 1948. The manner in which the transfer was to be made was to be decided during the next few months."[6] This meant two things: complete independence for India, but also that a capable Indian government had to be in place within a short amount of time (a year and a half), so that it could accept the responsibility. As Judd notes, "This meant that there had to be a transfer of power into responsible Indian hands by that date. In February 1947 it was not at all clear whose those hands might be."[7]

In addition to making this announcement, Attlee named Lord Louis Mountbatten as the new viceroy of India. The great-grandson of Queen Victoria, Mountbatten was not only a supporter of the Labour Party, but a nobleman. Because of his high stature and the level of respect he enjoyed in many parts of British society, he seemed like a good candidate to help the various parties involved negotiate Britain's withdrawal.

Mountbatten's job was to ensure a smooth transfer of power and to make sure a capable Indian government was in place by June 1948. As violence continued to erupt all over the country, however, Mountbatten came to understand the difficulty of his task. The Muslim League refused to back down on the partition of India and the formation of Pakistan, while Nehru and the Congress Party could not think of dividing the land of India.

Before long, Mountbatten came to accept that partition was the only solution, though Congress leaders continued to resist the idea. Although they were Hindus, many of them believed in a secular, democratic India that respected all religions. Gandhi himself opposed the idea of partition, saying, "My whole soul rebels against the idea that Hinduism and Islam represent two antagonistic cultures and doctrines. To assent to such a doctrine is for me a denial of God."[8] Despite their protests, Hindu leaders came to see that they had little choice in the matter. In April 1947, Nehru and Congress also surrendered to the idea of partition—as long as provinces that did not wish to join Pakistan would not be forced to do so. Disappointed that it had come to this point, Nehru sadly joked that by "cutting off the head we will get rid of the headache."[9]

Questions still remained: Where would the borders be drawn? So many provinces were mixed in terms of population (Muslim, Hindu, and Sikh), so where would these areas be relegated? What about areas like the northern province of Kashmir, which had a majority of Muslims but whose prince was a Hindu? What about the Sikh population of only 6 million people, which, as Yasmin Khan notes, "was almost evenly spread across the Punjab" and was worried about its solidarity?[10]

(continues on page 64)

LORD MOUNTBATTEN

A great-grandson of Queen Victoria, Lord Louis "Dickie" Francis Albert Victor Nicholas Mountbatten (originally Battenberg), Earl of Burma, was a dashing, charming member of the German aristocracy and the British royal family. Born on June 25, 1900, he was the second son of Prince Louis of Battenberg and Princess Victoria of Hesse and by Rhine. Prince Battenberg changed his name to Mountbatten after Great Britain went to war with Germany in 1914.

During World War I, Mountbatten joined the Royal Navy in 1916. During the early years of World War II, he served Britain as admiral of the fleet; his naval exploits were usually daring but had mixed success. Later, he was appointed Supreme Allied Commander of the South East Asia Theatre, a position he served in from 1943 until 1946 and in which he oversaw the defeat of the Japanese in their attempt to invade India and reconquer Burma.

When the war ended, Prime Minister Clement Attlee asked Mountbatten to serve as the new viceroy to India, knowing that Mountbatten was familiar with the region and its culture. Attlee also hoped that Mountbatten's considerable charm and popular personality would ease the British withdrawal from India and help the country remain intact.

Indeed, Mountbatten established solid relationships with Jawaharlal Nehru and Mohandas Gandhi. He and Nehru had much in common, and they became good friends. Mountbatten's personal life, however, had always been tumultuous and his marriage unstable. It is widely known, in fact, that Mountbatten's wife, Lady Edwina, had a romantic relationship with the charming and intelligent Nehru, of which her husband was most likely aware. Interestingly, it does not seem to have diminished Mountbatten's respect and affection for Nehru himself.

Mountbatten, however, had more trouble convincing Muhammad Ali Jinnah that a unified India was in the interest of the Muslim population. In the end, Mountbatten grew resigned to the partition of India into two states. When India became independent, Mountbatten served as its first governor-general for a short period of time. After he left India, he was named viscount and given the title Earl of Burma.

Mountbatten returned to naval life after his time serving in India. Lady Edwina died in 1960, and Mountbatten retired from the navy five years later. He spent time with their two daughters, Patricia and Pamela, to whom he was very close. On August 27, 1979, he was boating with his daughter, her husband, her mother-in-law, and his twin grandsons near his family summer estate, Classiebawn Castle, off the coast of Ireland. A bomb planted by the Irish Revolutionary Army (IRA) exploded, killing Mountbatten almost instantly, as well as one of his grandsons, his daughter's mother-in-law, and a local teenage boy whom Mountbatten had hired as a deckhand.

His assassination was a coup for the IRA, since they had executed a member of the royal family, and it sent shock waves throughout the world. Prime Minister Margaret Thatcher said of Mountbatten at the time: "His life ran like a golden thread of inspiration and service to his country throughout this century."*

---

* "Britain: A Nation Mourns Its Loss." *Time*, September 10, 1979. http://www.time.com/time/magazine/article/0,9171, 920606,00.html.

Mohandas Gandhi believed there should be no division between Hindus and Muslims in India. Gandhi is seen here embracing Muhammad Ali Jinnah, the leader of the All-India Muslim League from 1913 to 1947, in Mumbai, India, in September 1944.

(continued from page 61)

At one point, in May 1947, Mountbatten took Nehru— whom he considered a good friend—into his confidence, and showed the Indian leader a secret plan for division that had already been devised in London. The plans were probably more favorable to Pakistan, giving it more land than Nehru was comfortable with. Later, Nehru wrote to the viceroy that the plan had "produced a devastating effect upon me. . . . The whole approach was completely different from what ours had been and the picture of India that emerged frightened me . . . a picture of fragmentation and conflict and disorder, and, unhappily also, of a worsening of relations between India and Britain."[11] Since Mountbatten greatly respected Nehru, the plans continued to be revised. In June, a line to separate India and Pakistan was determined.

Continuing violence in June 1947, however, caused the British to speed up their plan to transfer power. On July 15, 1947, the India-Independence Act was passed. It declared that the transfer of power would take place in just one month, in August 1947—a full year earlier than originally planned. The act also declared that two new nations would be formed from the land of the Indian subcontinent: India and Pakistan.

The new transfer date necessitated rapid action. That month, Mountbatten informed the princes of several provinces—some of whom felt that they should declare independence rather than join either India or Pakistan—that they had to join one or the other. Later, they were promised, if a majority of their populations voted to drop out of the country, they could do so.

A TROUBLED PARTITION

Plans continued for partition, with Nehru and Jinnah arguing over which lands would be given to India and which to Pakistan. In recent years, it has come to light that the finalized plans, known as the Mountbatten Plan, were drawn up in a casual, careless fashion.

British lawyer Cyril Radcliffe had been tasked with going to India to chair the Indo-Pakistan Boundary Commission, which was to help draw the line between India and Pakistan, keeping in mind the sensitivity of the issue and the problem of mixed-population areas such as the Punjab and Bengal regions. Papers released in 1992 by the son of Christopher Beaumont, Radcliffe's secretary, show that the boundary was actually decided over a

(continues on page 68)

THE INDIAN INDEPENDENCE ACT OF 1947

An Act to make provision for the setting up in India of two independent Dominions, to substitute other provisions for certain provisions of the Government of India Act 1935, which apply outside those Dominions, and to provide for other matters consequential on or connected with the setting up of those Dominions.

18th July 1947

1 **The new Dominions.**

(1) As from the fifteenth day of August, nineteen hundred and forty-seven, two independent Dominions shall be set up in India, to be known respectively as India and Pakistan.

(2) The said Dominions are hereafter in this Act referred to as "the new Dominions", and the said fifteenth day of August is hereafter in this Act referred to as "the appointed day." . . .

6 **Legislation for the new Dominions. . . .**

(4) No Act of Parliament of the United Kingdom passed on or after the appointed day shall extend, or be deemed to extend, to either of the new Dominions as part of the law of that Dominion unless it is extended thereto by a law of the Legislature of the Dominion.

(5) No Order in Council made on or after the appointed day under any Act passed before the appointed day, and no order, rule or other instrument made on or after the appointed day under any such Act by any United Kingdom Minister or other authority, shall extend, or be deemed to extend, to either of the new Dominions as part of the law of that Dominion.

7 **Consequences of the setting up of the new Dominions.**

(1) As from the appointed day—

in size. A thousand miles separated East and West Pakistan, and it required several days to travel between them.

Most historians agree that the partition line, when it was finally determined, was very badly drawn. It divided some villages—and even some houses—in half and separated railways and waterlines. Radcliffe apparently was so deeply unhappy with the results that he hurried back to England afterward. But many historians believe that much of the blame for the chaos that followed partition rests with Mountbatten. "The viceroy, Mountbatten, must take the blame—though not the sole blame—for the massacres in the Punjab in which between 500,000 to a million men, women and children perished," Beaumont writes. "The handover of power was done too quickly."[12]

The chaos was indeed troubling and terrifying, and it did not bode well for the futures of either India or Pakistan. Nehru and Jinnah themselves begged Mountbatten to order British troops to curb the violence. According to historian Yasmin Khan, Nehru told the British viceroy, "Amritsar is already a city of ruins, and Lahore is likely to be in a much worse state very soon," while Jinnah said more directly, "I don't care whether you shoot Moslems or not, it has got to be stopped."[13]

Unfortunately, the violence only continued to escalate. Gandhi's peace activists and other groups that promoted peace among India's various factions tried valiantly to stop the violence, providing ambulance and medical services as well as trying to rescue minorities who were in danger of attack. The violence, however, was fueled by each group's uncertainty and fear regarding what would happen once India was divided.

A People Divided

Independence Day was set for August 15, 1947. In the weeks leading up to that date, the populations of Hindus, Muslims, and Sikhs living in the areas to be partitioned (Punjab and Bengal) grew desperately worried about the growing violence. Historian Yasmin Khan offers a vivid description of what people, terrified that they would wake up on the wrong and hostile side of the border, began to do:

> As Independence Day approached, life became nightmarish for people caught between the opposing sides. . . . Fear was the predominant emotion in the middle months of 1947, particularly in those districts of Punjab where inclusion in Pakistan or India was, as yet, unknown. . . . People experienced gradations of anxiety; some Punjabis felt paralysing

Muslim refugees wait to leave for Pakistan as they seek protected transport to Purana Qila, an ancient fort where many other refugees had gathered in the days before the final partition line was announced in August 1947.

and life-changing terror. In the worst-afflicted centres, in the hardest hit parts of Lahore and Amritsar, Rawalpindi and Sheikhupura, the most anxious took desperate measures—growing or cutting off their beards and learning the *Kalma* or Vedic phrases so that they could fake their religious identities if necessary. If possible, families sent their unmarried daughters away with guardians or relations, and decided upon hiding places in the roof spaces of barns or the small back rooms of temples or mosques. The optimists refused to take basic precautions but many minds turned to self-defence and the stockpiling of bags of sand and cooking fuel, and the collection of extra drinking water. Newly recruited watchmen patrolled villages and towns, and missiles and ammunition piled up.[1]

All this was taking place before the final partition line was even announced. The violence—with Hindus killing Muslims, Muslims killing Sikhs, etc.—continued to escalate. Between January and June of 1947, thousands had already been killed in the Punjab, and millions of dollars' worth of property and businesses destroyed. The British military did little to stop it, because its soldiers were preparing themselves to leave India for good and return home to England. Furthermore, the Indian regiments could not help because they too were being divided according to their religion: In the space of a few months, soldiers were being separated into a Pakistani army, consisting of Muslim soldiers, and an Indian army, consisting of Hindu soldiers. That separation rendered the whole military ineffective and unable to quell the growing violence.

The problem was that Mountbatten and his office would not reveal the exact partition line; indeed, that information was not revealed until *after* August 15. Although Mountbatten had a good sense of which lands he would award to each side, the debates continued and the boundary commission continued to deliberate other small details. The exact maps demarcating the two states were not actually ready until August 12. And even when they were finished, Mountbatten chose to keep them secret for a few more days, until after Independence Day had passed.

Nevertheless, people understood that the partition would fall in the Punjab and in Bengal and tried to guess where

Lord Louis Mountbatten, the last viceroy of India, is pictured at his desk in 1947. Mountbatten mistakenly believed that once people knew the border was clear and secure, they would move peacefully back to their original homes, even if they were now in the minority in the new states of India and Pakistan.

the exact lines would be drawn so that they could plan their futures. As Independence Day approached, a mass migration began: For example, in the Punjab, Muslims who realized they would be on the Indian side of the border packed up their belongings and moved west, while Hindus who saw that they would end up on the Pakistani side did the same, moving east. A small "trickle," which would soon turn into a "torrent,"[2] as described by Khan, began in the weeks before August 15. At first, Mountbatten, Nehru, and Jinnah and their constituencies did not worry about the people moving across the border. They assumed, as most of the migrants themselves did, that these people were moving only temporarily. They hoped that once the partition was clear, secure, and complete, everyone would feel safe enough to move back to their original homes, even if they might be living as minorities in that state. As the number of migrants grew larger and larger, however, it became clear that they were moving for good. Many of them sold their homes (even at a great loss) and transferred their money to banks or sent it to family members on the other side of the border. They were making plans to stay, in case they could never return.

When Independence Day finally arrived, it should have been a day that signified the glorious fulfillment of a centuries-old dream, but it came amidst some of the worst violence and hatred ever witnessed in the subcontinent. Because people were still not sure of where the lines were going to be drawn, and because there was no military in place to control the migration and help explain or confirm the demarcation, rumors exploded—some people heard that their village would fall to the other side, only to spend difficult days moving to another village, where they learned that the opposite was true. Others were paralyzed, not sure whether they should migrate or not, since a different day brought news of a different rumor.

Zealous nationalists on both sides perpetrated the killings. As young men were brutally killing, looting, and rioting, they justified it to themselves as their nationalist duty, a legacy of horror and brutality that would haunt India and Pakistan for decades after independence. As Khan explains, "the principal aggressors were paramilitaries composed of former soldiers and well-trained young men working hand in glove with the armed forces of the princely states. . . . Political interpretations of freedom, self-rule and power gave these men credibility and a sense of legitimacy."[3] But the real victims were the people of what would be Pakistan and India—the peasants and working-class people who cared only for the safety and survival of their families and communities.

By August 15, both Muhammad Ali Jinnah and Jawaharlal Nehru had been besieged by requests for help in migrating or for assistance in finding lost or kidnapped relatives. The two men, as well as Gandhi, were shocked and devastated by how their political planning had led people to suffer. Gandhi said, "This much I certainly believe—that [the] coming August 15 should be no day for rejoicing whilst the minorities contemplate the day with a heavy heart."[4] He chose to spend the day fasting and praying, rather that celebrating, and urged others to follow his lead.

For Nehru, the violence was like a nightmare come true. He had initially rejected the idea of separating India into two nations, one for Muslims and one for Hindus, because he believed that India should always be an inclusive country, open to all. According to Barbara and Thomas Metcalf, in the opinion of Nehru and his Congress Party, "India was not only successor to the Raj, but also a secular state, in which Muslims, with all other minorities, stood, in principle, on equal footing with their Hindu fellow citizens. Millions of Muslims, remaining behind after partition by choice or necessity, already lived within India."[5] Nehru had hoped that they would be one part of an India that was a mosaic of ethnicities and religions, not a Hindu-only nation. The violence was proving, however, that his vision was too idealistic.

Both India and Pakistan marked their independence. At midnight on August 14–15, in the first minutes of Independence Day, Pakistani radio stations announced the establishment of the state of Pakistan and included readings from the Koran. In India, Nehru delivered a speech that would become famous, in which he declared that India's soul, after centuries of colonialism, had finally found "utterance" and could express itself in freedom. All over the subcontinent, some families celebrated by sharing meals, candy, and songs, while others suffered in uncertainty, still fearing for their lives, not knowing how they would fare in whichever state they had found themselves.

NEHRU'S SPEECH UPON THE INDEPENDENCE OF INDIA, AUGUST 15, 1947

Jawaharlal Nehru, the first prime minister of India, was a gifted writer and orator, but many historians agree that no speech was as inspired as the one he delivered at the precise minute that India became independent from British colonial rule. The following is an excerpt from that speech:

Long years ago we made a tryst with destiny, and now the time comes when we shall redeem our pledge, not wholly or in full measure, but very substantially. At the stroke of the midnight hour, when the world sleeps, India will awake to life and freedom. A moment comes, which comes but rarely in history, when we step out from the old to the new, when an age ends, and when the soul of a nation, long suppressed, finds utterance. It is fitting that at this solemn moment we take the pledge of dedication to the service of India and her people and to the still larger cause of humanity.

At the dawn of history India started on her unending quest, and trackless centuries are filled with her striving and the grandeur of her success and her failures. Through good and ill fortune alike she has never lost sight of that quest or forgotten the ideals which gave her strength. We end today a period of ill fortune and India discovers herself again. The achievement we celebrate today is but a step, an opening of opportunity, to the greater triumphs and achievements that await us. Are we brave enough and wise enough to grasp this opportunity and accept the challenge of the future?

In whichever way independence was marked, violence erupted again a few days later, when the exact partition lines were revealed. The scale of migration rose exponentially as

Freedom and power bring responsibility. The responsibility rests upon this Assembly, a sovereign body representing the sovereign people of India. Before the birth of freedom we have endured all the pains of labour and our hearts are heavy with the memory of this sorrow. Some of those pains continue even now. Nevertheless, the past is over and it is the future that beckons to us now.

That future is not one of ease or resting but of incessant striving so that we may fulfill the pledges we have so often taken and the one we shall take today. The service of India means the service of the millions who suffer. It means the ending of poverty and ignorance and disease and inequality of opportunity. The ambition of the greatest man of our generation has been to wipe every tear from every eye. That may be beyond us, but as long as there are tears and suffering, so long our work will not be over.

And so we have to labour and to work, and work hard, to give reality to our dreams. Those dreams are for India, but they are also for the world, for all the nations and peoples are too closely knit together today for any one of them to imagine that it can live apart. Peace has been said to be indivisible; so is freedom, so is prosperity now, and so also is disaster in this One World that can no longer be split into isolated fragments.

To the people of India, whose representatives we are, we make an appeal to join us with faith and confidence in this great adventure. This is no time for petty and destructive criticism, no time for ill-will or blaming others. We have to build the noble mansion of free India where all her children may dwell.*

* Jawaharlal Nehru, "A Tryst with Destiny." August 14, 1947. http://www.fordham.edu/halsall/mod/1947nehru1.html.

people scurried across the newly revealed borders, carrying as many of their belongings as possible. It is estimated that 10 million people moved across the border in 1947, making it the largest mass migration in world history.

Unfortunately, the violence also rose. Historians agree that an ethnic cleansing took place in the Punjab and other parts of India and Pakistan, as militants grew determined to "cleanse" their now-demarcated regions of people from the "other" side. Estimates of the dead vary from a low of 250,000 to almost 1 million. The recurring and most haunting image of the partition-induced violence is the image of trains, arriving at their destinations in either country, carrying butchered corpses of once-hopeful migrants who had fled for their safety.

Both Jinnah and Nehru did their best to quell the violence. Jinnah told Pakistanis that they had to "make it a matter of our prestige and honour to safeguard the lives of the minority communities and to create a sense of security among them," while Nehru told Indians, "We have a Muslim minority who are so large in numbers that they cannot, even if they want to, go anywhere else" and that they must be protected.[6]

THE END OF AN EMPIRE

In 1942, Gandhi had famously told the British, "Leave India to God. If that is too much, then leave her to anarchy." It seemed in 1947 to be almost a prophecy and that anarchy would, indeed, rule the day.

After British soldiers finally left India and Pakistan in 1947, the violence continued to escalate to shocking levels in Bengal and in the Punjab. The international community was stunned by the scores of killings and their brutal nature. It was as if India's diversity had become its curse, with groups attacking one another on the sole basis of ethnicity, religion, or other dividing lines.

While people were being killed as they crossed borders into what they thought was safer territory, many regions beyond Bengal and the Punjab were mired in turmoil and uncertainty as well. While most princes of the 570 states that existed in the subcontinent had determined which nation to join, some had not. One of those rulers was the prince of Hyderabad, who was Muslim, although the majority of his people were Hindu. Since his state was completely surrounded by the territory of the new Indian state, it seemed most beneficial to join India, but the ruler refused. The Indian government gave him one year to make up his mind, and when he did not, the Indian Army invaded Hyderabad in September 1948 and forced it to join.

Kashmir, the home state of Nehru and his family, was another state that refused to join either side. Located high in the mountains of the Himalayas, it overlooked northern India as well as western Pakistan. Kashmir boasted a population of 4 million, most of which were Muslims. The prince of Kashmir, Hari Singh, however, was a Hindu who did not want to join either India or Pakistan. According to Wolpert, "As the countdown on Britain's transfer of power neared its conclusion, Hari Singh signed a standstill agreement with Pakistan, unable to bring himself to accede to either dominion and hoping that his mountainous state might be permitted to remain independent, a Switzerland of Asia."[7]

The location of Kashmir, situated between both countries, proved to be its main problem. Wolpert adds that while geographically, the prince would have done better to join Pakistan (because of the position of Kashmir in relation to the Indus River), he was worried that he would have trouble maintaining power in an all-Muslim state. A revolt of his own people in the fall of 1947, led by Muslim peasants who were supported by Pakistan, helped him to finally decide to join India. He formally joined Kashmir to India in October 1947, although Lord Mountbatten insisted that nothing could be formalized until the will of the Muslim majority was determined, once calm had been restored. In the end, the rebels took control

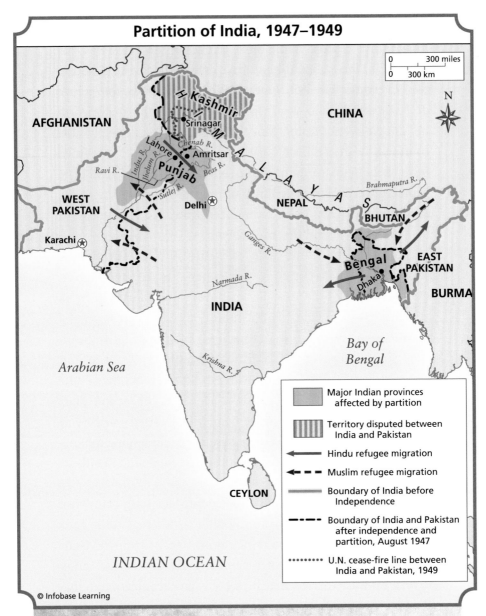

Partition of India, 1947–1949

0   300 miles
0   300 km

AFGHANISTAN

CHINA

N

Kashmir

Srinagar

HIMALAYAS

Chenab R.

Lahore

Amritsar

Indus R.

Jhelum R.

Punjab

Ravi R.

Beas R.

Sutlej R.

Brahmaputra R.

WEST PAKISTAN

Delhi

NEPAL

BHUTAN

Karachi

Ganges R.

Bengal

EAST PAKISTAN

Dhaka

BURMA

Narmada R.

INDIA

Arabian Sea

Krishna R.

Bay of Bengal

CEYLON

INDIAN OCEAN

Legend:
- Major Indian provinces affected by partition
- Territory disputed between India and Pakistan
- Hindu refugee migration
- Muslim refugee migration
- Boundary of India before Independence
- Boundary of India and Pakistan after independence and partition, August 1947
- U.N. cease-fire line between India and Pakistan, 1949

© Infobase Learning

The 1947 partition of India created the sovereign states of India and Pakistan. Pakistan was carved out of the Muslim majority regions, which included West Pakistan and East Pakistan (now Bangladesh), with India in between. India was created from the majority Hindu populations. The partition has long been criticized, because large groups fled their homes to find safety among their respective majority populations. Many political and ethnic tensions on the subcontinent can be traced to the partition.

of southwestern Kashmir, set up a government called Azad Kashmir ("Free Kashmir"), and joined Pakistan.

Jinnah and Nehru both issued demands that the other side withdraw its forces, as each claimed Kashmir for his own country. Thus was Kashmir divided. The disputed region would continue to cause problems and be the fuel for wars between India and Pakistan for decades to come. Hindu–Muslim hostilities, rather than be quelled by a separation of the nations, festered more dangerously than ever before.

8

A Series of Wars

Partition did not bring peace to the Indian subcontinent. The first war between India and Pakistan, also known as the First Kashmir War, occurred shortly after independence. It has its beginnings in October 1947, when the prince of Kashmir, Hari Singh, reluctantly acceded his state to India as a result of the Pakistani-supported rebellion in the western part of his state.

Each nation felt it had a right to the state of Kashmir. Pakistan thought Kashmir, with its majority Muslim population, should join its nation, since it had been established as the all-Muslim state in the subcontinent. India, led by Nehru (who had ancestral origins in Kashmir), wanted the state for its territorial advantage as well as historical and cultural ties. Many Kashmiris themselves, even some who were Muslim, wanted their state to remain independent.

A picture taken in October 1947 at the start of the First Indo-Pakistani War shows Muslim refugees fleeing to Pakistan while Hindus fled to India in the border city of Amritsar between the two countries. The conflict between Hindus and Muslims arose when Pakistan supported a Muslim insurgency in Kashmir.

The problem escalated when the Pakistani Army supported the rebels and formally invaded, trying to seize Srinagar, the Kashmiri capital. The Kashmiri military fought valiantly and succeeded in small ways, mostly in delaying the attack on Srinagar. Hari Singh, however, quickly sought help from India, which agreed to intercede only if Kashmir acceded to India. Under these difficult circumstances, Hari Singh formally joined Kashmir to India, and in exchange, he received military help to defend his borders.

The first official war between Pakistan and India began only two months after the British had withdrawn their forces from the subcontinent. Initially, the Indian forces did well, pushing back both the Pakistani military and the Kashmiri-Muslim forces, mostly because the enemy was unprepared for India's surprise entry. However, the Kashmiri winter was so cold and Indian soldiers were so unaccustomed to fighting in mountainous terrain that, as time wore on, they had less success.

While an end to the fighting was not visible, the United Nations sent in observers in the summer of 1948. A cease-fire was put into effect on January 1, 1949, almost 15 months after the initial fighting broke out. In the end, Kashmir remained divided: Pakistan now controlled 40 percent of Kashmiri territory, under the government of Azad Kashmir. Approximately 3,000 soldiers had died in the fighting (about 1,500 from each side). Despite the cease-fire, nothing had really been resolved. The continued uncertainty surrounding Kashmir's fate would lead to another war down the road.

In the meantime, things were progressing in India and Pakistan at different paces. Pakistan's Muhammad Ali Jinnah, known as *Qaid e Azam* ("The Great Leader"), died on September 11, 1948, in the midst of the First Kashmir War. His death heralded a period of trouble and conflict for Pakistan, because the nation lost in him a voice that understood its many problems and knew how to best accommodate and unify its many constituencies. Pakistan's main problems, according to historians, were how to govern a country that was divided geographically in two (East Pakistan in the Bengal region and West Pakistan in the Punjab region), as well as how to help Pakistan become a modern state without losing its Islamic character or the support of the more orthodox Muslim part of its population.

Without Jinnah, Pakistan struggled to find another leader who could help it move forward. Its first prime minister, Liaquat Ali Khan, was assassinated in 1951. In 1958, after a series of weak leaders, Pakistan's government was overtaken in a military coup led by General Muhammad Ayub Khan, who established himself in the office of prime minister. This period of martial law in Pakistan was tumultuous and also led it into its second war with India.

In India, on the other hand, Nehru's popularity boomed. According to Wolpert, "Panditji," as Nehru was nicknamed, ". . . was India's royal figure and its matinee idol, that unique combination of brilliance, good looks, and brooding isolation who endeared himself to admirers of both sexes and all ages throughout the land."[1] Because he was already well versed in relations with Western leaders, having served as the de facto leader of India even before its independence, he quickly moved to help India become a player on the world stage. He wanted to present India's best face to the world, as the planet's most populous democracy. He believed such a presentation would help lift his nation out of poverty and illiteracy, as well as bring about a more modern India.

The Congress Party, under Nehru's leadership, enjoyed immense popularity, mostly because of its inclusive vision of India. According to Metcalf and Metcalf, "The Congress Party under Nehru's leadership was committed . . . to the principles of secularism and socialism. Despite the predominance of Hindus among its membership, the Congress had always proclaimed itself a secular organization, and Nehru was determined that India should be a secular state."[2]

The prime minister's charisma and stature were enormously helpful to India's steady climb upward (in fact, Jinnah had enjoyed a positive international reputation as well, making one wonder if Pakistan's fate would have been different had Jinnah lived longer). Nehru became known for a work ethic and work habits that stunned others; he often worked late into the night and seemed inexhaustible. However, one of his many low points as prime minister was the assassination of Mahatma Gandhi in 1948. After Gandhi's death, Nehru continued Gandhi's mission, pushing for a secular India. In fact, before his death in 1964, Nehru had made it clear that he wanted to be buried in a secular manner, without religious ceremony or pomp.

THE SECOND INDO–PAK WAR

In 1964, after Jawaharlal Nehru passed away, his apparent successor was his daughter and only child, the quiet and apparently shy Indira, who had married Feroze Gandhi (no relationship to Mohandas Gandhi). For years, Indira had served as her father's companion, especially after the early death of Nehru's wife and Indira's mother. After Nehru's death, Indira was deemed too young and inexperienced to lead the Congress Party and the Indian government.

Instead, the Congress Party appointed Gulzarilal Nanda, who served as acting prime minister for two months before being replaced by Lal Bahadur Shastri in June 1964. For Shastri, his administration would be dominated by continuing problems with Pakistan, which was now led by its president, General Ayub Khan. (The office of prime minister of Pakistan disappeared under Khan's martial law.)

In the spring of 1965, shortly after India had emerged from a war with China in 1962 that left its military weakened, Pakistan made another attempt to seize territory in Kashmir. The Pakistani government's leaders reasoned that this was the perfect time to assert more control in the still-disputed region of Kashmir. They launched Operation Gibraltar, an attempt to send secret infiltrators into Kashmir to stir up rebellion. However, the operation was discovered and it failed.

In a speech celebrating India's independence that summer, Prime Minister Shastri claimed that Pakistan had invaded Kashmir, even though Zulfikar Ali Bhutto, the trusted adviser to Pakistan's Khan, denied the claim. Nevertheless, Shastri said, "force will be met with force and aggression against us will never be allowed to succeed."[3]

Then India attacked. Claiming to have been provoked by the infiltration of Kashmir, the government sent Indian forces to invade Azad Kashmir, the southwestern region of the state that was occupied by the Pakistanis. A savage battle ensued, which is known as the Second Kashmir War (1965), during which the air forces of both nations took part for the first time against each other. Pakistan's army fought back and launched a successful counteroffensive that captured the town of Akhnoor—an important strategic victory. One of the war's most decisive moments came in the Battle of Asal Uttar, during which the Indian Army's 4th Mountain Division crushed Pakistan's 1st Armoured Division, which was considered its strongest component. In January 1966, hostilities ended when the Soviet Union helped broker the Tashkent Agreement, which, as Metcalf and Metcalf explain, "restored the status quo before the outbreak of hostilities."[4]

THE THIRD INDO–PAK WAR

After the Tashkent Agreement, Prime Minister Shastri died. By then, Indira Gandhi, Nehru's daughter, was seen as having acquired sufficient political experience. She had served in Shastri's government and had traveled widely, exposing herself to international and domestic politics and bolstering her reputation as a worthy successor to her father. In 1966, she was appointed India's prime minister, one of the first women in the world to be named head of state of her nation.

Gandhi marketed herself as the "mother" of India and claimed to speak for the poor and voiceless; in fact, one of the campaign slogans she used was "*Garibi Hatao*" ("End Poverty").[5] However, she faced major problems during her long tenure as prime minister, such as class divisions, the threat of famine, and a continuing boom in population. She also allowed corruption to seep slowly into the workings of her administration.

Politically, she allied herself with the Soviet Union, which she believed was a necessary move, since the United States, which was then engaged in the Cold War with the Soviets, supported Pakistan with economic and military aid. Tensions

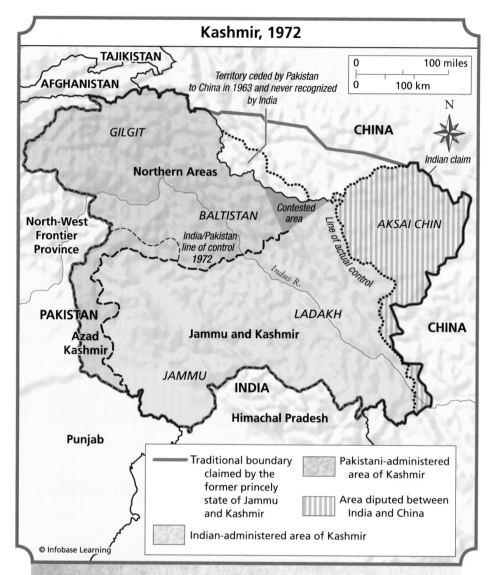

Kashmir, 1972

Kashmir has been the source of a dispute between India and Pakistan since the partition of India in 1947. In 1972, both countries agreed to a cease-fire at the line of control, which demarcates the unofficial border between the two countries. Despite the agreement, tensions still exist in present-day Kashmir. Pakistan has been accused of sponsoring militant activity in the area, while India's military presence is criticized.

between Pakistan and India continued during her administration, culminating in the Third Indo–Pak War in 1971.

For many years, West Pakistan and East Pakistan had had a difficult time solidifying their government, especially since they were separated geographically by India. Also, East Pakistan resented the fact that the government's power was concentrated in West Pakistan. On March 27, 1971, the East Pakistanis declared independence, claiming their own nation, to be called Bangladesh. With that, a civil war broke out, today known as the Pakistani Civil War or the Bangladesh Liberation War (1971). Pakistani leader Yahya Khan ordered the Pakistani military, the majority of which were from West Pakistan, to quell the Bangladeshi uprising in order to preserve the geographical map of Pakistan. During the suppression, however, many horrific acts of brutality and violence were committed against the people of East Pakistan. The violence only solidified the intent of the East Pakistanis to form their own country and be independent.

Though the primary battlefront was East Pakistan, India was affected by the civil war that was taking place on either side of its borders. After the war's outbreak, Indira Gandhi voiced the support of Indians for the East Pakistanis, but she did not send military aid. India did, however, open its eastern border to allow refugees to flee East Pakistan. As the numbers streaming across the border hoping for protection grew and grew, the refugee crisis became a tremendous burden on India's resources. Before long, the Indian military was stationed at the India–East Pakistan border.

India, under Gandhi, finally became involved in December 1971, when it was attacked by West Pakistan. The Pakistani government hoped to stop India from invading East Pakistan and helping the Bangladeshis succeed in their bid for independence. India retaliated, intending to stop Pakistan from crossing the border into western India. Again, India was in a difficult situation because it was located right betweeen the two regions of Pakistan.

India's air force quickly helped India gain an edge in the war. West Pakistan surrendered within two weeks. East Pakistan became Bangladesh, an independent nation. Other changes took place as a result of the joint success of India and Bangladesh: In West Pakistan, now known as Pakistan, the loss of so much territory was crushing. President Yahya Khan resigned from office and was replaced by Zulfikar Ali Bhutto. In India, Pakistan's defeat boosted the popularity of Indira Gandhi, who was now seen as having the strength necessary in times of crisis.

9

The Legacy of the Indian Independence Act

Since the last war between India and Pakistan ended in 1971, political tensions between the two nations have not eased. In addition, each nation has had its own turbulent political history, including a legacy of assassinations of its leadership.

In Pakistan, Zulfikar Ali Bhutto was a popular leader. He had gained political experience as the protégé of General Ayub Khan, Pakistan's former leader. However, a rift with Ayub Khan occurred in 1967, when Bhutto criticized one of the president's policies. The rift caused Bhutto to resign his post as foreign minister and a short time later form an oppositional party called the Pakistan Peoples Party (PPP), which soon became the most popular political party in the nation. The slogan of the PPP was "Islam our Faith, Democracy our Policy, Socialism our Economy."[1] Bhutto also promoted what he refered to as a "thousand year war with India" as one of the PPP's political platforms.[2]

Bhutto served as Pakistan's president from 1971 to 1973, after the resignation of Yahya Khan, and served as prime minister from 1973 to 1977. During his time in office, Bhutto made many controversial moves, including recognizing Bangladesh and attempting to establish normal relations with Indira Gandhi and India. One thing he did that would have far-reaching effects was to establish a nuclear program for Pakistan, eventually putting Abdul Qadeer Khan in charge of running and building the program.

Bhutto faced many challenges and growing unpopularity as the years progressed. In 1974, an oppositional leader was murdered, causing accusations to circulate about the underlying cause. In 1977, Bhutto and his regime were overthrown in a military coup led by General Zia ul-Haq. Martial law was imposed in Pakistan and Bhutto was arrested under charges that he had ordered the murder of the political leader. Though he was released after a short time because the evidence was found to be insufficient, he was arrested again in September 1977 and placed on trial for the murder.

The trial began in October 1977 and concluded in March the following year. During the course of the trial, shaky evidence was presented to connect Bhutto to the assassination. Most of the evidence was in the form of testimonies by people who claimed to be witnesses. Bhutto's opportunity to testify in his own defense was curtailed by a seemingly biased judge. In the end, Bhutto was declared guilty of conspiracy to murder and sentenced to death. Despite appeals for clemency from leaders across the world, he was executed by hanging on April 4, 1979. It is largely believed that the trial was corrupt from the start and was masterminded by General ul-Haq, who wanted to secure his own power by getting rid of his opposition.

In India, Indira Gandhi was also in political trouble, having grown very unpopular among mainstream Indians. In 1975, she declared emergency powers, giving her all-encompassing political authority. The now-infamous period, known as the "Emergency,"

(*Left to right*) Prince Philip, Gyani Zail Singh, Queen Elizabeth II, and Prime Minister Indira Gandhi greet each other at IGI Airport in New Delhi, during the royal couple's visit to India.

signaled a low point for India's democracy, in which free speech was suspended and all opposition was silenced. Many human rights violations occurred at this time, including a program in which many people were forcibly sterilized in order to stop India's booming population growth. Soon after the Emergency ended, Gandhi was ousted from power in 1977.

Gandhi returned to power in 1980, a year in which she faced problems in the Punjab with separatists who wanted an independent Sikh nation. In June 1984, Gandhi implemented Operation Blue Star and ordered the army into the Golden Temple, the holiest shrine for Sikhs, where guerrilla forces had holed themselves up. Wanting to end the conflict with the independence fighters once and for all, the army attacked the temple and its inhabitants. It is estimated that between 500 and 3,000 Sikh civilians, who were in the area to celebrate a religious festival, perished in the military action.

On October 31, 1984, as Gandhi left her home in New Delhi, heading out for an interview, she was shot and killed by Satwant Singh and Beant Singh, two of her own bodyguards. Both men were Sikhs and had been shocked by her actions during Operation Blue Star; the attack on the holy temple as well as the many deaths of innocent Sikhs had spurred the plot to assassinate her. The violence only continued in the days that followed: The Sikh community in India came under brutal attack by Hindus and other groups. Thousands of Sikhs were murdered and millions of dollars' worth of Sikh property destroyed.

Indira Gandhi was succeeded as prime minister by the elder of her two sons, Rajiv Gandhi (a younger son, Sanjay, had been killed years earlier in an accident). Rajiv sought to make the government transparent and avoid any semblance of corruption. The wave of hope that accompanied his leadership was aptly summed up by Rajiv Gandhi himself in a speech to the American government: "India is an old country, but a young nation, and like the young everywhere, we are impatient. I am impatient and I too have a dream of an India—strong, independent, self-reliant."[3]

Under Rajiv Gandhi's leadership, the Congress Party, which had flowered under the leadership of his great-grandfather Motilal Nehru and his grandfather Jawaharlal Nehru, became more popular than ever. Gandhi served as prime minister from 1984 to 1989; during his tenure, he worked hard to modernize India, especially in the technology sector. He also pushed to strengthen the Indian education system and to improve higher education in the country. In 1989, he left office under the cloud of a scandal, but two years later he was hopeful of a return to office. As he was campaigning in 1991, however, a terrorist suicide bomb killed him.

MORE VIOLENCE AND UNCERTAINTY

Just as Indira Gandhi had not continued the positive legacy of leadership established by her father, another political daughter inherited a similarly troubled legacy in Pakistan.

Zulfikar's daughter, Benazir Bhutto, became the leader of the PPP and eventually rose to the position of prime minister in 1988, making her the first female head of a Muslim nation. She served until 1990, when she was removed for alleged corruption; the charges claimed, among other things, that she laundered money and used her political status for financial gain. She made a successful comeback in 1993 and served as prime minister until 1996, when she was again forced to leave her position for the same reason.

Benazir Bhutto left Pakistan, returning only in October 2007 when President Pervez Musharraf granted her amnesty. She was greeted with a hero's return and immediately set about using her popularity to rebuild the PPP. She declared herself a candidate for the January 2008 elections. In December 2007, just two weeks before the elections, a bomb exploded during a rally for the PPP, killing her and many others. To this day, it is uncertain who was behind her assassination.

ECONOMICS ON THE SUBCONTINENT

In economic terms, India has been more prosperous than its neighbor and former sibling, Pakistan. In recent decades, prompted by former prime minister Rajiv Gandhi's technology and education initiatives, Indians have begun producing top-level, highly qualified, educated experts in many areas of science, technology, computers, engineering, and mathematics. For example, India produces software products and exports them to 95 countries around the world. Furthermore, according to the Embassy of India, "The Indian software industry has grown from a mere US $150 million in 1991–92 to a staggering US $5.7 billion (including over $4 billion worth of software exports) in 1999–2000. No other Indian industry has performed so well against the global competition."[4]

Furthermore, as much of the world economy has moved in recent decades away from a manufacturing-based one to a more knowledge-based economy, India has done well in following suit and making important adjustments to its workforce. For example, factory-trained workers are not in high demand these days, at least not as much as scientists, computer programmers, engineers, and people in other, similar professions. The Indian government and education system have kept pace with the changes in the economy and the needs of the workforce and have produced the types of workers who are in such demand. The Embassy of India claims, "India's most prized resource in today's knowledge economy is its readily available technical work force. India has the second largest English-speaking scientific professionals in the world, second only to the US."[5]

This ability to adapt has helped make India one of the most important emerging economies in the world today. It has also helped India fix many of its own domestic problems, which include a booming population and widespread poverty. India's current population is estimated to be 1.08 billion people, though a recent study by the Population Reference Bureau showed that it will most likely reach 1.63 billion and "overtake China as the world's most populous nation by 2050."[6] India's ability to keep unemployment rates low and its economy robust will be critical to lowering its poverty rate.

Another problem India faces internally is that of caste divisions; in recent years, despite rapid progress in the technology and science sectors, discrimination against the Untouchables continues to plague India's self-portrait as the world's largest democracy. Yet, because of the high demand for jobs in these new sectors, international companies that hire Indians are also hiring people in the other classes. A Microsoft executive recently described the problem: "We don't give a damn about any of these differences in caste or religion," he said. "It has made talent the number one issue for all companies."[7] This is good news for the Untouchables, who had been relegated to India's lowest-paid and most menial jobs for centuries. The demand for jobs has offered them an opportunity to rise up in social status and earn a better income. Yet they still face challenges in breaking through the barrier that separates the lower and middle classes. Because their caste is easily recognized by family names or hometowns, a company executive or administrator from a higher caste may not hire them. They also face problems in being admitted fairly into schools and universities because of the biases of enrollment officers. As India continues to modernize, it must face and address these problems.

While India still grapples with its own issues, it has done well overall for a nation so young. On the other hand, Pakistan has had a more difficult struggle—economically, politically, and culturally. Pakistan, like India, has a population boom, though its population growth is even higher than that of India. Reporter Sultan Shahin explains why:

> The reasons for this high growth rate are many. Apart from usual causes like extreme poverty and social insecurity, Pakistani society continues to suffer from medieval practices like early marriage of women and their poor education. Almost 50 percent of women in Pakistan are married before the age of 20, enormously increasing the chances of conception. In fact, the average fertility of women (number of live birth, per woman) in Pakistan is a high 6.1 compared to India's 3.7. Another factor is poor education of women. There is abundant evidence internationally that well-educated women, being career-oriented, generally bear fewer children.[8]

India has also done a better job than Pakistan of strengthening its educational system. Shahin notes, "The average literacy rate in Pakistan is a poor 35.7 percent compared to India's 49.9 percent. World Bank figures show that Pakistan's literacy rate is even lower than some of the countries of sub-Saharan Africa like Ghana and Nigeria. School enrollment rates in Pakistan are less than half the averages in India."[9]

While India is seen as an emerging superpower, Pakistan is still largely viewed as an impoverished nation with a stunted economy. According to a CIA overview of Pakistan, "Inflation remains the top concern among the public, jumping from 7.7% in 2007 to 24.4% in 2008, primarily because of rising world fuel and commodity prices. In addition, the Pakistani rupee has depreciated significantly as a result of political and economic instability."[10]

ISLAMIC FUNDAMENTALISM

Another major problem that Pakistan faces, on a cultural and political front, is the rise in radical Islamic fundamentalism. Generally speaking, such fundamentalists take on modernism as their chief enemy, arguing for a return to traditional religious practices and opposing the influences of reason and free thought. While Islamic fundamentalism has risen all over the world in recent decades, it takes different shapes in different regions. In Pakistan, which is considered a Muslim nation, fundamentalism has been influenced by the political situation within neighboring Afghanistan.

In Afghanistan, the Taliban ruled for many years, imposing severe social restrictions and interpreting Islam in a very fundamentalist way. The Taliban was ousted from power by the invasion of U.S.-led forces in 2001, but many of its leaders regrouped within Pakistan's borders. On May 1, 2011, al-Qaeda leader, Osama Bin Laden, was found and killed by U.S. Navy SEALs in a town in Pakistan. Terrorist groups such as al-Qaeda, which was responsible for the terror attacks on the United States on September 11, 2001, have long operated within Pakistan's borders.

In 1999, Pakistan's government was toppled by a military led by General Pervez Musharraf. While Musharraf initially thought that the main issue of his presidency would be the still-contested region of Kashmir, it soon became the problem of Islamic fundamentalism. Fundamentalists in Pakistan, for example, wanted to impose strict sharia, or Islamic, law. Many fundamentalists interpret the law to include such tenets as the forced veiling of women, death sentences for those who commit crimes such as adultery and robbery, and the execution of homosexuals.

In order to defeat the Taliban in neighboring Afghanistan, where the 9/11 attacks had been orchestrated, the U.S. government needed Pakistan's help and turned to Musharraf as an ally. Under pressure from the U.S. government to crack down on the growing fundamentalist movement, Musharraf made a number of moves that risked the support of the Pakistani people, many of whom previously had a favorable attitude toward fundamentalism and the implementation of Sharia law.

In March 2007, Musharraf suspended Chief Justice Iftikhar Muhammad Chaudhry from the court, which led to major protests. Chaudhry had accused the administration of corruption and refused to resign from his post, as Musharraf wanted him to do. The move was very unpopular, forcing Musharraf to reinstate the judge.

In July of that same year, Musharraf ordered the military to storm the Red Mosque in Islamabad, where fundamentalists were operating. The disastrous attack led to the deaths of 100 people. Across the nation, fundamentalists clashed with military forces in retaliation, leading to attacks on the government and on innocent civilians in the form of suicide bombings. Musharraf's popularity continued to sink, while criticisms of his government by Chaudhry and others escalated.

In November 2007, Musharraf worried that the court would declare his recent reelection unconstitutional. He then declared a state of emergency, suspended the Constitution of Pakistan

(continues on page 102)

A.Q. KHAN

In 1998, India and Pakistan conducted tests of nuclear weapons, making it clear to the world that both nations possessed nuclear capability. This knowledge has made other nations nervous, because of the instability of Pakistan's government and the rising threat of fundamentalism within its borders.

Former prime minister Zulfikar Ali Bhutto, who helped establish a nuclear program in Pakistan as a way of ensuring that the nation stayed apace with other countries, also installed nuclear scientist Abdul Qadeer Khan as the head of developing Pakistan's nuclear capabilities. However, A.Q. Khan, as he is popularly known, exploited the nuclear program in ways that have stunned other countries.

Khan was born in 1936 to an Indian-Muslim family that moved to Pakistan in 1952. When Khan was a child, a fortune-teller apparently told his mother that her son would grow up to be a very important person: "He will outstand in his family and will be a source of great pride and honor to his parents, brothers, and sisters. He is going to do very important and useful work for his nation and will earn immense respect."*

His father, a supporter of the Muslim League, believed his son should have a thorough education. Khan was educated at the University of Karachi and later pursued graduate studies at the University of Leuven and later at the Delft University of Technology where he earned a Ph.D. in metallurgical engineering. During later work in the Netherlands, he was accused of stealing nuclear secrets from a facility there. When he was found out, the authorities let him go and he returned to Pakistan.

On February 6, 2009, Pakistani nuclear scientist A.Q. Khan talks to the media outside his residence in Islamabad. Khan admitted to leaking nuclear secrets to Iran, North Korea, and Libya during his time as head of the Pakistani nuclear program.

Bhutto put Khan in charge of the uranium enrichment program (enriching uranium is a necessary step toward developing nuclear power and weaponry) in 1976. Shortly afterward, the new Pakistani leader General Zia ul-Haq gave Khan more power, and the nuclear laboratory was renamed the Khan Research Laboratories (KRL). Under Khan's leadership, Pakistan developed its nuclear program, culminating in successful weapons tests in 1998.

In 2004, it was revealed that Khan had been selling nuclear secrets to other governments, including North Korea, Libya, Iran, and others. Khan confessed to running the black-market network, but President General Musharraf pardoned him because Khan was considered to be a national

(continues)

(continued)

hero. World governments wanted the chance to question Khan themselves, but this was blocked by Pakistan, which placed him under house arrest for several years as a way of proving that it had dealt with the problem. Musharraf's actions, however, brought the Pakistani government under suspicion that it had known about Khan's activities.

In early 2008, Secretary of State Hillary Clinton of the United States said of the Pakistani scientist: "With respect to A.Q. Khan, there's no doubt he is probably the world's greatest proliferator. The damage that he's done around the world has been incalculable."**

Khan, who was discovered to be suffering from cancer, was released from house arrest in 2008. In February 2009, a high court in Pakistan released Khan and allowed him free movement inside the country. The United States and other nations continue to fear that a freed Khan will continue to be a nuclear proliferation risk.

---

* William Langewiesche, "The Wrath of Khan," *Atlantic Monthly*, November 2005. http://www.theatlantic.com/magazine/archive/2005/11/the-wrath-of-khan/4333/.
** "Pak Must Give Access to A.Q. Khan: US Lawmakers." Pakistan Defence. http://www.defence.pk/forums/national-political-issues/23265-pak-must-give-access-q-khan-us-lawmakers.html.

(continued from page 99)

and the Parliament, and essentially imposed martial law on the nation. Chaudhry and other judges were arrested and placed under house arrest, while political chaos and outrage over Musharraf's desperate actions ensued. Chaudhry became the voice of Pakistanis who demanded justice in the political system. From his home, he wrote an open letter declaring, "I will fight till the last drop of my blood to save the Constitution of Pakistan."[11] During his time under house arrest, he was visited by Benazir Bhutto and given the support of the PPP, but Bhutto's assassination a month later only increased the political tension in the country. In August 2008, Musharraf resigned as president and was succeeded by Asif Ali Zardari, Benazir Bhutto's widower.

FUNDAMENTALISM IN INDIA

Many of these problems relate to India. For years, Islamic fundamentalists operating from within Pakistan conducted terrorist attacks on the neighboring, largely Hindu nation. In December 2001, terrorists attacked the Indian Parliament building in New Delhi, killing seven people. The audacious attack shocked Indians, and the blame was immediately placed on the Pakistani government for not restricting and controlling the actions of fundamentalist groups within its borders. Pakistan's inability to control terrorism, it seemed, was proving to be a threat to its secular neighbor.

Tensions between the two nations soon escalated. Both India and Pakistan amassed troops on their borders in a standoff that caught the attention of the entire world, especially since both nations had become nuclear powers in 1998. During the tense standoff, Pakistan conducted missile tests as a form of intimidation and several skirmishes led to the deaths of soldiers and civilians alike. The standoff was eventually resolved without a full-scale war, but the problematic relationship between the two nations had been greatly damaged.

Then, in November 2008, terrorists, believed to have originated from Pakistan, attacked the city of Mumbai (formerly Bombay), the financial capital of India, stunning the nation and the world. The attacks were conducted on a number of fronts. For several days, hostages were held inside the Taj Mahal Palace Hotel, while parts of the hotel burned. In other parts of the city, bombs went off, killing people. Terrorists also targeted and killed specific civilians, such as a rabbi and his wife who ran a Jewish center known as the Nariman House. Blame immediately fell on Pakistan, and it was later confirmed that the terrorists belonged to Lashkar-e-Taiba, a Pakistani-based organization that had played a role in the 2001 attacks on the Indian Parliament as well.

Despite the ongoing tensions and occasional outbreaks of violence over key issues (including the fact that Kashmir continues to be a contested region), the majority of people in Pakistan and India hope for a better future and improved relations between their two countries, which are, after all, siblings that are separated by a legacy of colonialism and the Indian Independence Act of 1947.

CHRONOLOGY

1600	The British East India Company is granted a charter to work in India by Queen Elizabeth I; the following year, the company opens the spice trade between India and Europe.
1698	The new East India Company is granted a charter by King William III.
1708	The old and new East India Companies merge as the United Company.
1857-1858	The Indian Mutiny lasts 18 months.
1858	The British Crown establishes the Raj and assumes sole authority in India.
1861	India Civil Service (ICS) is established by the Raj; opportunities for Indians are restricted at first.
1885	The Indian National Congress (later Congress Party) is established.
1905	Bengal is partitioned by Viceroy Curzon.
1906	The Muslim League is established.
1914-1918	England (and India) are involved in World War I.
1914	Gandhi returns to India.
1919	Gandhi leads his first satyagraha in pursuit of Indian independence.
1935	The Government of India Act is passed.
1939-1945	Great Britain is involved in World War II.
1942	"Quit India" movement led by the Congress Party.
1946	Massacres in Calcutta.
1947	Lord Mountbatten becomes viceroy of India. Indian Independence Act is passed, dividing India into two

dominions: India and Pakistan. Massacres and mass migrations follow the partition, which takes effect on August 15.

1947-1949   First Indo–Pak War.

1948   Gandhi is assassinated by a Hindu radical.

1965   Second Indo–Pak War.

1971   Third Indo–Pak War.

1979   Pakistani former prime minister Zulfikar Ali Bhutto is executed.

1984   Indira Gandhi is assassinated by her Sikh bodyguards.

TIMELINE

1858
The British Crown establishes the Raj and assumes sole authority in India.

1906
The Muslim League is established.

1919
Gandhi leads his first satyagraha in pursuit of Indian independence.

1600

1919

1600
The British East India Company is granted a charter to work in India by Queen Elizabeth I; the following year, the company opens the spice trade between India and Europe.

1914
Gandhi returns to India.

1885
The Indian National Congress (later Congress Party) is established.

1998   India and Pakistan conduct nuclear tests, proving that each has nuclear weapons capabilities.

1999   Indo–Pak conflict at Kargil. Pakistani government is toppled by a military coup led by General Pervez Musharraf.

2007   Benazir Bhutto is assassinated weeks before elections in Pakistan.

2008   Terrorist attacks on Bombay, plotted by Pakistani operatives.

1942
"Quit India" movement
led by the Congress Party.

1935
The Government of
India Act is passed.

1948
Gandhi is assassinated
by a Hindu radical.

1935   1998

1947
Lord Mountbatten becomes viceroy
of India. Indian Independence Act
is passed, dividing India into two
dominions: India and Pakistan.
Massacres and mass migrations
follow the partition, which takes
effect on August 15.

1998
India and Pakistan
conduct nuclear
tests, proving that
each has nuclear
weapons capabilities.

NOTES

CHAPTER 1

1. Denis Judd, *The Lion and the Tiger: The Rise and Fall of the British Raj.* New York: Oxford University Press, 2004, p. 124.
2. Ibid., p. 127.
3. Ibid., p. 128.

CHAPTER 2

1. Stanley A. Wolpert, *A New History of India.* New York: Oxford University Press, 2004, p. x.
2. P.J. Marshall, *Problems of Empire: Britain and India, 1757–1813.* Sydney, Australia: Allen & Unwin, 1968, p. 16.
3. Ibid., p. 15.
4. "Passage to India," PBS, http://www.pbs.org/empires/victoria/text/historypassage.html.
5. Judd, p. 75.

CHAPTER 3

1. Judd, p. 74.
2. Ibid., pp. 84–85.
3. Ibid., pp. 86–87.
4. Wolpert, p. 239.
5. Ibid., p. 241.
6. Ibid., p. 243.

CHAPTER 4

1. Arthur B. Keith, ed., "Lord William Bentinck on the Suppression of *Sati,* 8 November 1829," in *Speeches and Documents on Indian Policy, 1750–1921.* Oxford: Oxford University Press, 1922, vol. 1, pp. 208–226, http://www.fordham.edu/halsall/mod/1829bentinck.html.
2. Judd, pp. 89–90.
3. Wolpert, p. 250.
4. Ibid., pp. 252–253.
5. Ibid., p. 253.
6. Ibid.
7. Quoted in Wolpert, p. 259.
8. Ibid., p. 273.
9. Wolpert, p. 258.
10. Ibid., p. 264.
11. Ibid., p. 263.

CHAPTER 5

1. M.K. Gandhi, *Non-Violent Resistance (Satyagraha).* New York: Schocken Books, 1961, p. 7.
2. Praveen Swami, "Jallianwala Bagh Revisited," *Frontline.* Vol. 14, No. 22, November 1–14, 1997, http://www.hinduonnet.com/fline/fl1422/14220500.htm.
3. Quoted in Wolpert, p. 204.
4. Judd, p. 149.
5. Ibid.
6. "Historic Figures: Mohammad Ali Jinnah," BBC, http://www.bbc.co.uk/history/historic_figures/jinnah_mohammad_ali.shtml.

CHAPTER 6

1. Quoted in Judd, p. 198.
2. Ibid., p. 168.
3. Judd, p. 172.
4. Quoted in Wolpert, p. 344.

5. Wolpert, p. 347.

6. Rajni Kothari, *Politics in India.* New Delhi, India: Orient Longman Private Limited, 1970, p. 73.

7. Judd, p. 179.

8. Quoted in Thomas Pantham and V.R. Mehta, *Political Ideas in Modern India: Thematic Explorations.* Thousand Oaks, Calif.: SAGE, 2006, p. 231.

9. Quoted in Wolpert, p. 347.

10. Yasmin Khan, *The Great Partition: The Making of India and Pakistan.* New Haven: Yale University Press, 2007, p. 109.

11. Quoted in Judd, p. 183.

12. "Partitioning India Over Lunch," BBC News, http://news.bbc.co .uk/2/hi/south_asia/6926464.stm.

13. Quoted in Khan, p. 107.

CHAPTER 7

1. Khan, pp. 112–113.

2. Ibid., p. 123.

3. Ibid., p. 131.

4. Ibid., p. 151.

5. Barbara D. Metcalf and Thomas R. Metcalf, *A Concise History of Modern India, Second Edition.* New York: Cambridge University Press, 2006, p. 225.

6. Khan, p. 157.

7. Wolpert, p. 353.

CHAPTER 8

1. Wolpert, p. 351.

2. Metcalf and Metcalf, p. 233.

3. Quoted in Wolpert, p. 375.

4. Metcalf and Metcalf, p. 249.

5. Ibid., p. 253.

CHAPTER 9

1. "Pakistan," Country Studies, http://countrystudies.us/ pakistan/19.htm.

2. Ibid.

3. India Today, "10 Quotes That Said It All," http://indiatoday. intoday.in/index.php?issueid= 23070&option=com_content& task=view&sectionid=36.

4. Embassy of India, "India's Information Technology Industry," http://www.indianembassy.org/ indiainfo/india_it.htm.

5. Ibid.

6. "India population 'to be biggest,'" BBC News, http://news.bbc .co.uk/1/hi/world/3575994.stm.

7. Paul Beckett, "Caste Away: India's High-Tech Revolution Helps 'Untouchables' Rise," *Wall Street Journal*, June 23, 2007, http:// defeatpoverty.com/articles/Caste %20Away%20-%20WSJ.pdf.

8. Sultan Shahin, "India vs. Pakistan: Contrasts in Social Development," *The Observer of Business and Politics*, April 14, 2000, http://www.hvk.org/ articles/0400/30.html.

9. Ibid.

10. Central Intelligence Agency, *The CIA World Factbook 2010.* New York: Skyhorse Publishing, 2009, p. 521.

11. "Iftikhar Muhammad Chaudhry," Biographicon, http://www.biographicon.com/ view/se4j4.

BIBLIOGRAPHY

Beckett, Paul. "Caste Away: India's High-Tech Revolution Helps 'Untouchables' Rise." *Wall Street Journal*, June 23, 2007. Available online. URL: http://defeatpoverty.com/articles/Caste%20Away%20-%20WSJ.pdf.

"Britain: A Nation Mourns Its Loss." *Time*. September 10, 1979. Available online. URL: http://www.time.com/time/magazine/article/0,9171,920606,00.html.

Central Intelligence Agency. *The CIA World Factbook 2010*. New York: Skyhorse Publishing, 2009.

Embassy of India. "India's Information Technology Industry." Available online. URL: http://www.indianembassy.org/india info/india_it.htm.

Gandhi, M.K. *Non-Violent Resistance (Satyagraha)*. New York: Schocken Books, 1961.

"Historic Figures: Mohammad Ali Jinnah." BBC. Available online. URL: http://www.bbc.co.uk/history/historic_figures/jinnah_mohammad_ali.shtml.

"Iftikhar Muhammad Chaudhry." Biographicon. Available online. URL: http://www.biographicon.com/view/se4j4.

"India population 'to be biggest.'" BBC News. Available online. URL: http://news.bbc.co.uk/1/hi/world/3575994.stm.

India Today. "10 Quotes That Said It All." Available online. URL: http://indiatoday.intoday.in/index.php?issueid=&id=2 3070&option=com_content&task=view&sectionid=36.

"Indian Independence Act 1947." The National Archives. Available online. URL: http://www.legislation.gov.uk/ukpga/Geo6/10-11/30.

Judd, Denis. *The Lion and the Tiger: The Rise and Fall of the British Raj*. New York: Oxford University Press, 2004.

Keith, Arthur B., ed. "Lord William Bentinck on the Suppression of *Sati*, 8 November 1829." In *Speeches and Documents on Indian Policy, 1750–1921*. Oxford: Oxford University Press, 1922, vol. 1. Available online. URL: http://www .fordham.edu/halsall/mod/1829bentinck.html.

Khan, Yasmin. *The Great Partition: The Making of India and Pakistan*. New Haven: Yale University Press, 2007.

Kothari, Rajni. *Politics in India*. New Delhi, India: Orient Longman Private Limited, 1970.

Langewiesche, William. "The Wrath of Khan." *Atlantic Monthly*. November 2005. Available online. URL: http://www.theatlantic .com/magazine/archive/2005/11/the-wrath-of-khan/4333/.

Marshall, P.J. *Problems of Empire: Britain and India, 1757–1813*. Sydney, Australia: Allen & Unwin, 1968, p. 16.

Metcalf, Barbara D., and Thomas R. Metcalf. *A Concise History of Modern India, Second Edition*. New York: Cambridge University Press, 2006.

Nehru, Jawaharlal. "A Tryst with Destiny." August 14, 1947. Available online. URL: http://www.fordham.edu/halsall/mod/ 1947nehru1.html.

"Pak Must Give Access to A.Q. Khan: US Lawmakers." Pakistan Defence. Available online. URL: http://www.defence. pk/forums/national-political-issues/23265-pak-must-give- access-q-khan-us-lawmakers.html.

"Pakistan." Country Studies. Available online. URL: http:// countrystudies.us/pakistan/19.htm.

Pantham, Thomas, and V.R. Mehta. *Political Ideas in Modern India: Thematic Explorations*. Thousand Oaks, Calif.: SAGE, 2006.

"Partitioning India Over Lunch." BBC News. Available online. URL: http://news.bbc.co.uk/2/hi/south_asia/6926464.stm.

"Passage to India." PBS. Available online. URL: http://www.
pbs.org/empires/victoria/text/historypassage.html.

Shahin, Sultan. "India vs. Pakistan: Contrasts in Social Development." *The Observer of Business and Politics*, April 14, 2000. Available online. URL: http://www.hvk.org/articles/0400/30.html.

Swami, Praveen. "Jallianwala Bagh Revisited." *Frontline*. Vol. 14, No. 22, November 1–14, 1997. Available online. URL: http://www.hinduonnet.com/fline/fl1422/14220500.htm.

Wolpert, Stanley A. *A New History of India*. New York: Oxford University Press, 2004.

FURTHER RESOURCES

BOOKS

Keay, John. *India: A History*. New York: HarperCollins, 2000.

Malik, Iftikhar H. *The History of Pakistan*. Westport, Conn.: Greenwood Press, 2008.

WEB SITES

India–Pakistan Timeline. BBC News.
  http://news.bbc.co.uk/hi/english/static/in_depth/south_
    asia/2002/india_pakistan/timeline/default.stm

The Future of Kashmir? BBC News.
  http://news.bbc.co.uk/2/shared/spl/hi/south_asia/03/
    kashmir_future/html/default.stm

PICTURE CREDITS

INDEX

ABOUT THE AUTHOR

SUSAN MUADDI DARRAJ is Associate Professor of English at Harford Community College in Bel Air, Maryland. She completed her master's degree in English literature at Rutgers University–Camden and has authored several titles for Chelsea House. Her book of short fiction, *The Inheritance of Exile*, was published in 2007 by University of Notre Dame Press, and she currently serves as senior editor of the literary journal *The Baltimore Review*.